YOUTH,
HUMANISM,
&
TECHNOLOGY

YOUTH, HUMANISM, & TECHNOLOGY

KEVIN D. KELLY

Basic Books Inc., Publishers

NEW YORK   LONDON

B+I 750 |525| 11|1|72

PREFACE

In these days of change and uncertainty, it is difficult to determine what is mainstream sociology and what is not. This book does not necessarily meet the specifications of conventional sociology, but I believe this reflects the state of the discipline as much as the state of the book. The perspective one brings to a sociological analysis is at least partially determined by the environment in which one exists. My own orientation reflects a positivist grounding during graduate training, modified by a critical analysis of this interpretation during the turmoil of the late sixties. I concluded that some of the conventional wisdom of sociology consisted only of unproven assumptions that had been taken for granted for so long that they had taken on the appearance of truth.

The meaning of terms such as "alienation" has changed over time and has lost its original critical nature. Other terms, such as "modernization," have become almost magical and are used as explanations of other phenomena.

The reader should be aware that this book reflects my own orientation, which is partially a result of the society in which I live, just as his or her reading of the book will be affected by the perspective that he or she brings to the reading.

I have attempted to bring together some of the recent criticisms of modern industrial societies and some of the explanations of the rise of oppositional youth movements within such societies. A synthesis of this kind necessarily owes much to the ideas of others. Especially important have been the writings of Peter Berger, Richard Flacks, Louis Kelso, Snell and Gail

Putney, Philip Slater, and Robert Theobald. I acknowledge my debt to these authors and apologize to them where I have used their ideas to support conclusions with which they might not agree. Their ideas have been changed by my own interpretation of them.

Besides the ideas of other authors, the argument developed here is a result of long conversations in which ideas were tried out, altered, and brought together—important to thank are Marion Steele, Elaine Thomas, and Allen Wannebo. Good friends should share the credit for the strengths of a book and also the responsibility for its weaknesses. After all, they had a great influence upon the perspective through which I see the world.

East Lansing, Michigan   KEVIN D. KELLY
April, 1972

CONTENTS

YOUTH,
HUMANISM,
&
TECHNOLOGY

ONE

The Universal Fake-Out:
The Self in Industrial Society

In order to understand the current behavior of youth, it is necessary to look at the conditions that exist in industrial societies that might produce such behavior. Generally, large amounts of "deviant" behavior in a society suggest that something is wrong with the institutions (patterns of behavior) in that society, and that in some way these institutions do not allow satisfaction of human needs.

In attempting to explain the emergence of large amounts of deviant behavior in a society, two perspectives can be taken. Which of these the analyst starts with will determine what type of analysis he will do, what factors he will look for, and ultimately, what conclusions he will reach. If one starts with a conception that states either that there are no basic human needs and that human beings can therefore adapt to any existing social order, or that an existing social order allows satisfaction of what needs there are, one will then seek to determine why some individuals or groups are unable to "adjust" to the existing social order. Explanations that start from this first conception generally look for some psychological reasons why persons are unable to adjust and may conclude that the deviants are rebelling against their fathers or have some other personal "problem" of adjustment. Similar types of explanations might be cast in a sociological mold and may assert that something in the person's environment "caused" his inability to adjust. Most of these explanations are deterministic in that they look for some "cause" of the problem behavior. Explanations cast in this first perspective are essentially conservative in nature and tend to reaffirm the validity of the existing order.

A second perspective assumes that there are autonomous human needs that "provide an independent basis with which to compare societies to each other, as more or less consonant with basic human needs" (Etzioni, 1968, p. 878). This perspective leads one "to expect pressure to change existing societies and cultures toward more responsive ones" (Etzioni, 1968, p. 878). This perspective is further likely to assume that social change comes about through the actions of conscious, striving human beings as they attempt to make sense of the world. This approach is likely to be phenomenological and is also likely to be radical in that, in attempting to determine if an existing order allows satisfaction of human needs, it is likely to raise questions about the basic assumptions of that order.

It is important to keep in mind when reading any analysis of a social movement—such as present-day youth movements—which perspective is being used, since this is likely to influence greatly the type of conclusions that are reached. This is especially important in dealing with the behavior of youth in modern industrial societies, the topic with which this book is concerned.

In recent years there has been much discussion of the meaning and significance of the present youth movements and the emergence of a youth culture or "counter-culture." The crucial points that analyses of the counter-culture attempt to resolve are 1) what factors in advanced industrial societies produce youth movements of the type that were thought to be characteristic only of modernizing societies, and 2) whether the youth culture is in some way a sign that industrial societies are going through or are about to go through a significant change or transition in values and form.

The question whether or not youth movements reflect a general social and cultural change in advanced industrial societies generates a great deal of heat. This is because, even among "objective" social scientists, we are talking about changes in the social reality in which we exist. One can observe the changes in modernizing societies with a reasonable amount of objectivity, but discussions of changes in our own society lead to the proponents of differing views calling each other ideologues and insisting that one or the other interpretation of youth movements is value-free and scientific, while the opposing position is ideological. As Becker (1966) has noted, in such situations the sociologist can only recognize that his position is not value-free and then proceed to do his research and analysis as objectively as possible.

With this in mind, then, we can proceed with an analysis of the emergence and meaning of a youth culture or counter-culture in modern industrial societies. The perspective I will use here is the second of those mentioned above: the phenomenological perspective. That is, I am starting with the assumption that "there is a universal set of basic human needs which have attributes of their own which are not determined by the social structure, cultural patterns, or socialization process" (Etzioni, 1968, p. 871). Essentially, I am contending that there are "basic *human* needs which are universal but whose foundation is not biological" (Etzioni, 1968, p. 873). I will attempt to show how these needs arise from the human tendency to construct social reality through interaction. I will then examine industrial societies in an attempt to determine the extent to which their membership is able to satisfy these needs. This analysis will be mainly concerned with American society but might also apply to other mature industrial societies. I will then examine the possibility that the present youth culture emerged as a result of a gap between basic human needs and the ability of industrial societies to allow satisfaction of these needs.

The Emergence of Human Needs

Because of the biological world-openness of the human organism, human needs are very general. Essentially, we can place the needs of the human animal in two categories: physical needs and self needs (Putney and Putney, 1964, pp. 18–36).

Physical needs are those that are necessary for the continued functioning of the organism. They include the needs for food, water, air, etc. Needless to say, if a society does not provide these needs, it will cease to exist. Also, as long as the ecological condition of a society is such that these needs are difficult to satisfy, they will be the predominant concern of the society.

An additional group of physical needs are the general ones which are the driving force of the organism: a general need for physical activity, a general need for mental activity, and a general need for sexual activity (referred to here in the biological sense only). Since these needs are general, they can be satisfied in any number of different ways. Thus, the need for sexual activity, can be satisfied by heterosexual activity, homosexual activity, masturbation, etc. The limits on which activities will be allowed will be socially determined. Most societies provide for these physical needs to some extent, although social institutions vary greatly in the quality of the satisfaction they allow.

The physical needs of human beings are similar to the needs of other animals. Humans differ primarily in the general nature of these needs and in the fact that a much wider range of possible ways of satisfying these needs exists in the human organism. The needs of men take on their distinctly human character only in a consideration of the self needs.

The emergence of mind and the development of self are the key factors which differentiate men from other animals. Mind and self are not things; they are processes which arise through the relationship of men to the social world (Mead, 1934). Man is not born with a self. The self develops as the human organism interacts with the social world and with persons within the social world. The crucial element in being a self is the ability of the human organism, through the use of symbols, to be an object to itself by reflection.

As the human child interacts with other persons in the social world, he develops a conception of self by using others as social mirrors so as to see himself as they see him. The reaction of others to the emerging self is determined by taking the role of the others and assuming the attitude of others toward oneself. Thus, a fundamental characteristic of the self is getting outside oneself—the self can be both object and subject.

The self-concept is an elusive sort of entity. Persons are not born with a self-concept, but rather develop one through interaction with other persons. It is difficult for a person to determine who he is, for in order to do so, he must get outside himself and see himself as others see him. Humans do this by "taking the role of the other": by using the reactions of others to their behavior as social mirrors and forming a conception of self from what they see in those mirrors. This suggests that the self never exists in isolation from the social environment in which it is formed. Often, we tend to look at our relationship with the environment as being a matter of what is in here versus what is out there. But, the self-concept can only be formed through an interaction between what is in here and what is out there. The self is never fixed but, rather, varies depending upon the environment in which a person exists.

There are two self needs that arise through the process of developing a self-concept through social interaction (Putney and Putney, 1964, pp. 23–36). These needs come about because of the way the self-concept is formed through man's relation to the social world.

The most general of the self needs is the need to develop an accurate and acceptable self-concept. That is, a person's socially produced identity must reflect what he is as a biological

organism, and what he perceives himself to be must be acceptable in terms of his society's version of reality as reflected in the
social mirrors of significant others. If social institutions do not
generally permit accuracy or acceptance of the self-concept,
then those institutions will leave unfulfilled an important human
need. Further, if a person's self-concept is to accurately reflect
what he is, the social reality of the society in which he lives
must have an image of an acceptable human being that is reasonably consonant with what human beings actually are. If the
image of acceptability or "straw man" that exists in a society,
bears little or no resemblance to any human being, then an
accurate and acceptable self-concept will be difficult to develop.

An additional self-need that is closely related to the first is
the need to develop and expand the self through interaction
with other human beings. This need is best satisfied in conditions of "intimate association"—interaction in which human
beings reveal all or most of what they are to other human
beings. Intimate association appears to be necessary if persons
are to develop an accurate and acceptable self-concept. Thus,
these two needs are closely linked and come about in the process of developing a self through interaction. With this in mind,
we can turn to a consideration of how well these needs are satisfied in modern societies.

To determine whether or not he is acceptable, an individual
compares the image of himself that he sees in the social mirrors, with his society's vision of what an acceptable person is.
If that picture of an acceptable person were consistent with
what most human organisms actually are, it would probably not
be too difficult to develop an accurate and acceptable self-con-
ception. However, in industrial societies (and perhaps in all societies that have existed up to this time), the version of an acceptable person is not consistent with the reality of human
organisms. The human organism is capable of a wide range of
behavior and thought. Only some of this behavior and some of
this thought is acceptable in any given society. Societies con-

struct images of acceptable human behavior that exclude much of the range of behavior of which humans are capable. All human beings have the ability and sometimes the desire to engage in murder, rape, and a wide range of unacceptable sexual behavior. Also, most human beings are not nearly as efficient nor as knowledgeable as social roles require them to be.

The image that industrial societies have of an acceptable person, then, is a straw man. Further, an underlying assumption exists that acceptable persons do not have unacceptable desires (Putney and Putney, 1964). However, since the image of what is acceptable is a social myth, all persons do have unacceptable desires. If a person were to openly reveal all parts of himself, the reactions of others that he would see in the social mirror would be very unfavorable, and the person would not be able to form an acceptable conception of self.

Consequently, starting early in life, humans learn to hide parts of themselves in order to obtain favorable reactions from others. Children learn that their parents reward them, love them, and react favorably toward them when they hide unacceptable thoughts and desires. When they reveal themselves honestly, they are punished, love is withdrawn, and the social mirror shows an unacceptable person. Thus, persons learn to project a "public self" in order to obtain favorable reactions from others.

As any sociologist knows, the occupant of any position in a society performs a role which goes with that position. That role consists of expectations for behavior. Goffman (1959) looks at this roleplaying in terms of performances and of the problems involved in maintaining a performance so as to convince others that you are what you wish to appear to be. A doctor must give a performance to convince his patients that he has a vast store of medical knowledge and is capable of solving their ills (even if he isn't). An executive must convince others in his firm that he works extremely hard and is the driving force behind the firm (even if he doesn't and isn't). An officer must convince the enlisted men who are following him that he knows what he is doing so that they will follow him into combat (even if he doesn't). A professor must convince his students that he actually knows something that they don't.

This does not mean that inept occupants of these positions have to perform while capable ones don't. Regardless of a man's capability and the degree of his acceptance of the values that go with a position, he must appear to be even more capable and more committed. No one is going to feel comfortable being operated on by a doctor who is a mere human, who is unsure of himself, who must make guesses as to what is the right thing to do, etc.

A performer may play a role cynically or may come to believe in the role he is playing. The performer is aided in convincing others that he is what he pretends to be by the props that go with his position. There is the setting (plush offices and secretaries help to form the impression that the executive is busy and important). There is also the personal front (clothing, posture, expressions, etc.).

How many times have we gone to see an important person and had to get past several secretaries before entering the domain of the great man? How often have we stood and waited while he finished some important task before looking up to acknowledge our presence? Of course, he must appear to be busy when we enter even if he actually hasn't been doing a thing. Otherwise, the whole image that he wishes to project would collapse. Likewise, the bride must wear white even if in fact she is not a virgin. The important thing is that she appear to be.

Other rituals help to foster the impression that great skill is necessary to fill a position and that the occupant of that position possesses such skill. Long training periods are often required to fill a position even if it does not actually take that long to acquire the necessary skills. The long training period is very impressive. Thus, since it generally requires four years of medical school to become a doctor, four years of preparation are also provided for dentists and pharmacists even though they could be trained in less. Stiff qualifications are usually announced for entry into a position while nearly anyone may actually be accepted. A reading of a college catalogue would convince most people that it requires tremendous intelligence and hard work to get a degree and an almost inhuman capacity to get a graduate degree. Of course, anyone who has been through these programs knows that the actual training isn't nearly so tough (unless he has come to believe the role he is playing). The important thing is that outsiders don't know. They may suspect, but they aren't sure, and that is all the edge a performer needs.

Most performances serve to reaffirm the moral values of the community. That is, our values say that occupants of important positions must be efficient and capable so we perform to maintain those values. Further, these performances extend into all areas of human life. Hardly anyone will admit openly to masturbating since that would destroy the moral value that such behavior is wrong and would also imply that an individual could not obtain other forms of sexual satisfaction. So, despite the fact that everyone masturbates, pluralistic ignorance keeps most people believing that most others do not. Likewise, most people would never admit that they engage in wild, pornographic sexual fantasy, although everyone does. One wonders why we bother with pornography laws when any individual is perfectly capable of inventing his own fantasies (including your nine-year-old kid).

Since the public self excludes those elements of the human organism that do not fit the social straw man, reactions to the public self are generally positive, and the image that a person sees in the social mirror is an acceptable one. If this were all there was to the process, developing an acceptable self-concept would not be particularly difficult. Unfortunately, there is more to the process.

Although the only part of a person that others see is the public self, the other (unacceptable) parts are still there. When persons do not reveal parts of themselves to others, they anticipate the reactions they would receive if they did reveal these parts. Since the social mirror in this case consists of the straw man, the anticipated reactions of others are negative. So, the self-concept formed from anticipated reactions of others to the "private self" is unacceptable. Consequently, the person is not able to form an acceptable self-concept. He receives favorable reactions to his public self but anticipates unfavorable reactions to his private self.

We begin to see here what an interesting and tragic game we play. Each person in an interactive situation is projecting a public self that is the only part of the person that each of the others sees. The public selves revealed by each of the participants are the stuff from which the straw man is made. Since all of the persons are playing the same game, they all succeed in fooling each of the others, and we have a "universal fake-out." Each person is in the position of comparing his private self with all its faults and unacceptable desires with the public selves of each of the others. In these circumstances each individual can only lose and wind up finding himself unacceptable. Since all are playing the same game, all find themselves unacceptable. Thus, it is not possible for persons within such a social system to develop either an accurate or an acceptable self-concept. The need is not satisfied, and so each person continues desperately to try to satisfy that need. But since he is not aware of the nature of the need, his attempts to satisfy it only lead him to more grief.

Not being aware of what his real needs are and having learned to project a public self to gain acceptance, the normal American attempts to deal with his feelings of unacceptability by projecting a more desirable public self: not being able to obtain direct self-acceptance by revealing all of himself to others, he attempts to gain indirect self-acceptance (Putney and Putney, 1964, pp. 63–74) by improving his public performances.

Since attempts to gain indirect self-acceptance do not deal with the need to find the entire self acceptable, such attempts fail, and the person continues to work on improving his public performance without ever being able to find himself acceptable.

Since this whole game that we play is misdirected, it continues indefinitely without ever getting anywhere. Persons seek more and more money, prestige, status, and other symbols of acceptability that will improve their public images. This search for indirect self-acceptance becomes the driving force that keeps a consumer-oriented modern industrial society running. More and more useless production is supported because the goods produced become important symbols in the indirect search for acceptance by improved public image. Since the process is based on a false image and is heading nowhere, it goes on indefinitely.

A society and its ability to satisfy human needs can be characterized as "authentic," when the appearance and the underlying structure are both responsive to basic human needs; "alienating," when both the appearance and the structure are unresponsive; and "inauthentic," when the underlying structure is unresponsive but an institutional or symbolic front of responsiveness is maintained (Etzioni, 1968, p. 881).

There is some question whether there has ever been a truly authentic society. Perhaps this condition is only a utopian dream. Perhaps such a society is possible, but only at some future time when human beings are fully self-aware and able to construct social institutions consonant with human needs. I will discuss this problem later. For the moment, we will assume that modern industrial societies, at any rate, are not authentic.

Alienating societies would be those where there exist rather open conditions of slavery, large differences in power and wealth, and work conditions which clearly do not meet human needs. There have been many societies which might fall in this category, and most analyses of early industrial societies stress their alienating character.

But what about modern industrial societies, and especially American society? Etzioni (1968) suggests "that it is a mark of the post–World War II industrialized societies that they devote a major part of their endeavors to 'front' activities." That is, advanced industrial societies are inauthentic in that they present images of full participation and of meeting human needs, but do not actually allow participation or satisfy needs. Thus, "one can make a fairly strong case that there is a trend toward less outright exclusion and more reliance on pseudo-participation through societal-managerial techniques in various specific societal institutions as divergent as work, education, and politics" (Etzioni, 1968, p. 883). Universities are especially adept at creating illusions of participation through departmental advisory committees, academic councils, and other "representative" devices.

I have suggested in this chapter that the illusions created in the social realities of advanced industrial societies do not allow satisfaction of the need for an accurate and acceptable self-concept or the need for intimate association. Further, a great deal of energy goes into creating images through a universal fake-out. If this is so, it would certainly suggest that social movements might arise which would attempt to alter this condition. Before looking at these movements, however, it will be helpful to look at the process through which social reality is created and to examine how advanced industrial societies reached their present condition.

TWO

Out of Touch with Reality: Creating Reality through Social Interaction

In order to analyze the development of industrial societies and their institutionalized patterns of behavior, I will attempt to combine an ecological perspective with a phenomenological one.

When we look at human life on earth from an ecological perspective, we start with the assumption that ways of life are a function of conditions of life (Duncan, 1964). Life depends on materials available in the environment. Such materials are used over and over again following a circular path through the ecosystem. However, this flow of materials is accomplished only if work, an expenditure of energy, is done. As work is done, the ecosystem loses potential energy, which is replenished from outside. The law of conservation holds between materials and energy: the total supply of materials and energy is fixed, although one can be converted into the other.

The active agents in the use of materials and energy on earth are human beings. Strangely, this obvious fact is often overlooked or downplayed by proponents of the ecological perspective. Since use of energy and materials by human beings must be patterned and directed, instructions on how energy is to be expended—knowledge—are needed. Unlike materials and energy, the supply of knowledge is not fixed. Instead, knowledge tends to increase, resulting in virtually limitless transformations of materials and energy.

Knowledge, then, refers to the cultural environment that is created by human beings through symbolic communication. It includes all those rules that human beings create to pattern and bring order to their activities. The creation of social institutions, then, results from the unique ability of humans to use symbol systems for storing and using knowledge.

During the course of human evolution, man developed the ability to use symbol systems and create culture. This in turn greatly affected man's physical evolution. That is, dependence on culture patterns has been a continuous selective force favoring the development and perpetuation of an ability to adjust to the human type of social life (Duncan, 1964, p. 48). This style of life revolves around interaction with other human beings through the use of symbolic communication. Through this interaction, humans create culture patterns and institutions that in turn affect the future development of human societies.

The range of behavior in other animals is determined largely by instincts. During the course of human evolution, however, the human animal became less and less affected by instincts and more and more affected by socially constructed patterns of behavior. Humans evolved into animals characterized by a biologically intrinsic world-openness (Berger and Luckmann, 1966, pp. 48–50). That is, the human animal, not being limited and controlled by instincts, is capable of a wide range of behavior. Humans are born relatively early in the process of physical development and develop in an interrelationship with their environment. This includes both the physical environment and the symbolic environment, which is created by man.

Since the human organism does not biologically provide stability for conduct, man exists in a state of anomie or chaos. There is no intrinsic order in the world inhabited by human beings. Because of man's biological nature and his capacity to use symbols in interaction with other men, he will attempt to impose order on a chaotic universe by developing social institutions to pattern and order his behavior (Berger and Luckmann, 1966, pp. 51–53). Through interaction, men construct a social environment. The limits of this environment are set by the physical environment in which man exists, but once constructed, this socially constructed environment acts on the physical environment. Thus it does not make sense to say that human organization is a dependent variable determined by the physical environment and technological development, as some ecologists are inclined to conclude. The relationship between social organization on the one hand, and the physical environment and technology on the other, is dialectical, with each affecting and imposing limits on the other.

Through externalization of their attempts to make sense of a chaotic universe, men impose order on the world and transform their biological world-openness into a relative world-closedness (Berger and Luckmann, 1966, p. 51). It should be emphasized here that any patterns of human behavior are not fixed and are constantly being created and changed through human activity. Further, both social organization and technology are created by men and then both affect and limit the future behavior of men. Social reality reacts on the men who created it by taking on a "solid" appearance through objectification.

The objective reality of society is a process and not a stable and unchanging facticity. That is, social reality is a continuing process of objectification, which is defined as the perception of phenomena as part of a physical external world whose existence is independent of our consciousness of it. The process of objectification first involves the habitualization of behavior as man experiences and deals with his environment. As this habitualization increases, man begins to develop typifications of behavior (and hence of other men), which and who in turn develop reciprocal typifications. As these processes continue to develop, the expectations of behavioral responses become defined as 1) correct because they are validated by one's experience (that is, are in line with one's typifications) or 2) incorrect because they are challenged by one's experience (that is, not predicted by one's typifications). Thus is introduced the concept of legitimations. Certain ways of acting are legitimately acceptable, hence real, while other ways of acting are relegated to the realm of "unreality" or fantasy. People therefore tend to assume those roles which may be expected of them (that is, defined as real). With the introduction of a descendant generation unaware of the habitualizations, etc., which have preceded them, these roles and their attendant functions take on even more facticity, since alternative realities are inaccessible.

When a particular group creates a pattern of activity or social institution, that institution has a tenuous objective character. However, when the institution is passed on to the next generation, it takes on a more solid or objectively real character. Since the next generation had no part in creating and shaping the social world, it seems to be a given reality. Through this process of objectification, institutions appear as self-evident, unalterable, and real. The institution no longer appears as something created by men as one of a number of possible alternatives, but rather takes on the character of something with an existence independent of men, imposed upon them from outside. The social world that man has produced is experienced as something other than a human product. It is this character of social institutions which gives them a built-in alienating potential. Man becomes alienated from that which he has created by seeing it as something imposed upon him.

While social institutions take on an objective character as they are passed from generation to generation, they also must be explained and justified (Berger and Luckmann, 1966, p. 61). Consequently, elaborate ideologies are created to justify existing institutions and increase the self-evident nature of existing patterns of human behavior. The main justification for existing institutions generally comes from religious ideology, which acts as a "sacred canopy" that gives the entire social world the appearance of having been created by some superhuman external being (Berger, 1969). This greatly increases the objectivity of the social world. Other ideologies, such as those developed by the social sciences, also tend to reify existing institutions.

It may be seen that the process is one of institutionalization. Each habitualization, each typification takes on a stability previously nonexistent that 1) provides opportunities to develop more effective communication of their social reality and 2) more greatly objectifies and defines these realities. Institutions and institutional relationships result then from the stability of expectations and understandings which one experiences throughout life. The roles people assume in relationship to these institutions, depend on the reality they have experienced. Also, within these roles, as the results of stabilized typifications, universes of symbolic understanding may be developed. One's actions take on meaning, first in relationship to this social reality, later in relationship to other meanings that, through the same process, have become objectified as social reality. Legitimation here begins to take on its most concrete objectiveness. One's response to the reality around him defines him (and his actions) as legitimate contributions to his society or as unacceptable and undesirable aliens to the culture in which he exists. The machineries and social organization of systems of symbolic universe maintenance are covered extensively in Berger and Luckmann (1966, pp. 104–128). Mythology, theology, philosophy, and science are predominant among the systems of maintenance recognized.

It is not so much that given institutional patterns of behavior develop according to an ideological plan, but rather that patterns of behavior develop in any number of ways, including accidentally, and then are justified by ideologies that are constructed later. Since the institutions in any society will represent only a narrow sphere in the total range of possible human behavior, a new generation will always ask, "Why do we do it this way?" Some explanation is needed so that the institutions do not become transparent.

The ideologies that develop are based on a number of assumptions. Each statement in an ideological chain is based on some underlying assumption, which may in turn be based on another underlying assumption. Over a period of time the statements in an ideological chain take on a self-evident quality. Since no one questions a statement, people become unaware that it rests on underlying assumptions. If someone does get to the underlying assumption, it too has a self-evident quality. Generally, at the bottom of any institutional pattern is some assumption about "human nature." The particular way of behaving in a particular society becomes "human nature." Thus, we hear statements such as "Man is a competitive animal" instead of "Given the institutional patterns of present industrial societies, man tends to behave competitively." Since given institutional patterns are seen as resting on human nature, it is, of course, silly to talk about making fundamental changes in these patterns.

A relatively simple chain of assumptions can be seen in the following exchange on the subject of pornography:

GOOD CITIZEN: Let's get that filth off the newsstands and out of the bookstores!
CYNIC: Why?
GOOD CITIZEN: Because youngsters might get their hands on it.
CYNIC: And suppose they do?
GOOD CITIZEN: It's bad for them.
CYNIC: In what way is it bad for them?
GOOD CITIZEN: It will arouse them.
CYNIC: How does being aroused harm a child?

At this point the discussion has reached a point where it is necessary to examine the underlying assumption on which an entire set of accepted statements rests. In this case, studies show that arousal is quite harmless. However, the point is that the discussion would rarely ever get to the underlying assumption in order to attempt to determine whether or not it was true. Each statement made by the "good citizen" is viewed as a self-evident truth, and most people would not ask the question which follows each self-evident truth.

When we consider that most people would never follow the above chain to its conclusion, we can see why more complicated institutional patterns such as the family, the educational system, or the economic system become reified. As we noted in Chapter One, the universal fake-out exists because people are unaware of the assumption that acceptable persons do not have unacceptable desires. Rarely does anyone mention that our entire educational system, from grade school to graduate school, is based on the assumption that learning is uninteresting. Strange things happen when institutions become reified.

Because of the world-openness of the human organism, men construct a social world through interaction with other humans. This social reality, which exists only because humans continue to create it, becomes seen as something which has an existence independent of its human creators. Often the institutions in a society become ends in themselves rather than means to such ends as the satisfaction of human needs.

The social reality that men construct is precarious. Anything that threatens to undermine the ideologies that legitimize social institutions has the potential to destroy the institution. Any alternative version of reality is dangerous because it implies by its very existence that a present reality is not based on the nature of man and is not inevitable (Berger and Luckmann, 1966, p. 106). If the alternative version of reality exists only in the minds of a few individuals, it can be dismissed as fantasy, and the persons who expound it can be told to "get back in touch with reality." However, if a reasonably large number of people begin to act and interact on the basis of an alternative version of reality, their actions could make the official reality transparent. Institutions, after all, do not exist independently of the human beings who externalize themselves by creating social worlds. When human beings begin to interact on the basis of different perceptions of reality, institutions change or disappear.

Thus, societies will attempt to bring back into the fold those deviants who appear to be escaping to another reality. This is generally done through a process of "therapy."

Therapy entails the application of conceptual machinery to ensure that actual or potential deviants stay within the institutionalized definitions of reality, or, in other words, to prevent the "inhabitants" of a given universe from "emigrating." . . . Since therapy must concern itself with deviations from the "official" definitions of reality, it must develop a conceptual machinery to account for such deviations and to maintain the realities thus challenged. This requires a body of knowledge that includes a theory of deviance, a diagnostic apparatus, and a conceptual system for the "cure of souls." [Berger and Luckmann, 1966, p. 113]

Men create social institutions by externalizing their interpretations of the universe through interaction with other men. As these institutions are passed on from generation to generation, they take on a real, solid appearance through objectification. Any generation, then, is raised in interaction with both a physical environment and a symbolic social environment. Since the human organism is not limited by instincts to given patterns of behavior, its wide possible range of behavior will be limited through an internalization of the social world. This occurs in the process of developing a self.

Since the reactions of others to a person's behavior will be determined by the patterns of behavior recognized as valid in a given society, through the process of developing a self, the human child internalizes the social world. At the same time, by externalizing his interpretations of the world through action, each human being is creating and modifying social reality.

The self, then, is the connecting link in a pair of dialectical relationships: an external relationship between the individual organism and the social world, and an internal relationship between the individual's biological substratum and his socially produced identity (Berger and Luckmann, 1966, p. 180). Since the self is involved in both these relationships, it should be apparent that the individual organism and its environment are both part of the same process and are not two separate things. However, it usually seems as though the individual is separate from his environment and is in conflict with its environment. This occurs because it is possible for alienation to take place in either of the relationships mentioned above. The individual can become alienated from the social world, and the individual's biological nature can become alienated from his socially produced identity. The second of these alienations occurs through the process I have called the universal fake-out.

There is a close relationship between the process of becoming alienated from parts of the self through the universal fake-out and the process of becoming alienated from existing social reality through "reification." Reification is:

the apprehension of human phenomena as if they were things, that is, in non-human or possibly suprahuman terms. Another way of saying this is that reification is the apprehension of the products of human activity as if they were something else than human products. . . . Reification implies that man is capable of forgetting his own authorship of the human world, and further, that the dialectic between man the producer, and his products is lost to consciousness.

. . . as soon as an objective social world is established, the possibility of reification is never far away. . . . Reification can be described as an extreme step in the process of objectification, whereby the objectified world loses its comprehensibility as a human enterprise and becomes fixated as a non-human, non-humanizable, inert facticity.

Both the institutional order as a whole and segments of it may be apprehended in reified terms. . . .

Roles may be reified in the same manner as institutions . . . reification of roles narrows the subjective distance that the individual may establish between himself and his role-playing. Finally, identity itself (the total self, if one prefers) may be reified, both one's own and that of others. There is then a total identification of the individual with his socially assigned typification. He is apprehended as *nothing but* that type. [Berger and Luckmann, 1966, pp. 89–91]

When an individual defines himself totally in terms of the social roles he is playing, he is acting in "bad faith" and has become alienated from these aspects of the self which are not consistent with his socially assigned typification.

I have suggested that there are human needs which exist because of the process through which human beings create social reality and develop a self-image. Earlier, I discussed two of these needs and the problems that persons have satisfying them in modern American society. These were the need for an accurate and acceptable self-image, and the need to verify this self-image and expand the self through association. We can now add a third general need: the need to verify this self-image and expand the self through action (Putney and Putney, 1964, p. 27).

As I have emphasized throughout this chapter, the active agents in the use of materials and energy in the ecosystem are human beings. As the existentialists have pointed out, man must act in order to be, and what he becomes is largely the summation of his actions. Since it is through his actions that man creates both technology and social reality, if he is to act as a conscious, striving, self-aware human being, he must have reasonable control over his activity. If, through the process of reification, men see their own products as alien, their activity has become alienated and is no longer free. Likewise, to the extent that a man's activity is controlled by other men, it is not free. There are obviously degrees of control, ranging from nearly absolute control, as in the case of slavery, through the more subtle controls which exist in modern industrial societies. In the next two chapters, I will discuss the problem of alienated activity in industrial societies.

It should be kept in mind that the three human needs I have discussed in this book are related. As Putney and Putney note:

24

These three needs are closely interrelated; in fact they can be separated only analytically. Through actions in association with others, the individual develops a self and forms a self-image. This self-image can be found acceptable only if he has confidence that it accurately reflects the self, and such verification is established through further action and association. The process cannot be short-circuited by self-deception; manipulations of the self-image which are not verified through action and association leave the individual with the fear that his self-image is a fraud and that lurking behind it is an unacceptable self. [1964, p. 36]

I have discussed the possibility that satisfaction of human needs may be thwarted through alienation of men from the products of their creation and alienation from aspects of the self that are not consistent with a socially assigned typification. The extent to which either or both of these alienations occurs will depend on the type of social institutions men create as they expand their niche in the ecosystem. Since I am concerned here with the question of these alienations in industrial societies, I will examine some specific patterns of behavior as they developed and exist in industrial societies. I will be especially concerned with the social organization of the activity of work.

THREE

The Great Full Employment Hoax: The Reification of Work in Industrial Society

Human needs, which are very general, are of two types: physical needs (for food, water, oxygen, shelter, etc.), and self needs (to develop an accurate and acceptable self-concept, to expand the self through interaction with other humans, and to expand the self through action). Since the human organism cannot survive if its basic physical needs are not met, these would be expected to take first priority. When the basic needs are satisfied, we might expect the self needs to be the primary human concern. With this in mind, we can look at the way in which humans attempt to satisfy their basic needs. Since satisfaction of the basic needs is uncertain in man's natural environment, most of the activity of human beings up to the present time has been an attempt to deal with the production and consumption of wealth. This effort reached a point of great success with the emergence of capitalism and the value-system associated with it, and with the Industrial Revolution, leading to our present system of industrial capitalism.

There are two factors in any system of production: the human and the nonhuman. The human factor consists of man's labor, both manual and intellectual. The nonhuman factor originally consisted of resources in the natural environment, such as productive land, animal power, etc. As human history unfolded, the power and skills of machines were added to this nonhuman factor.

Through externalization, human beings create material items (tools, technology) and nonmaterial items (institutions). The institutions that humans create pattern and direct their use of natural resources, energy, and technology; these institutions also determine how the right to consume what is produced, is distributed.

In order for human beings to satisfy their basic needs (that is, to consume wealth), they must, of course, produce wealth. That much usually seems obvious. What often is overlooked, however, is that production cannot occur unless institutions provide some way for the wealth that is produced to be consumed. Up until the beginning of industrial societies (about 1800) this probably was not an important concern, since scarcity was a fact of life and demand for wealth always exceeded supply. That is, there was more than enough demand for whatever was produced.

Until 1800 human societies were essentially laborist: human productive power and skill was the main force in the production of wealth (Kelso and Adler, 1958, pp. 87–90). It was through his labor that man produced, and it was through his labor that he earned the right to consume. In village or tribal societies, land was usually owned by the group, with each man owning his own labor. In civilized laborist societies, slave owners or feudal lords came to own the land and often also the labor of other men. By owning slaves, who would produce to satisfy their basic needs, some men were able to concentrate their activity on filling their self needs throught art, politics, philosophy, etc. This does not mean that humans always recognized their self needs or worked to satisfy them (a look at some of human history suggests that they did not), but the opportunity existed only when the basic needs were satisfied.

27

Human societies thus consisted of a leisure class and a working class.

Humanistic movements (such as parts of the American Revolution) stressed the need for each family to own its own land so that a man would not have to work for the benefit of someone else. Only if he could use the products of his own labor could a man enjoy freedom. As long as there was plenty of land (such as on the American frontier) the dream of an agrarian democracy made some sense. As long as production was primarily a result of human labor, a distribution of wealth through human labor made sense and the overall economic system remained balanced.

However, the supply of land is fixed and human populations have expanded greatly. Also, the industrial revolution brought machines into the production process, so that the basic balance between production and consumption began to alter. First of all, the appearance of machines greatly increased the production of wealth. One would expect that this might lead to the end of scarcity and the general satisfaction of basic needs for all men. However, this obviously didn't happen, at least partly because the reification of human institutions prevented men from using their technology to meet their needs.

The value-system associated with capitalism (scarcity, work, guilt, authority, rationality, commitment) emerged over a long period of time, between the twelfth century and the Industrial Revolution. This value-system, or worldview, emerged as a response to growth in the division of labor and a form of social organization requiring the accumulation of surplus. Our present pattern of institutional values developed as a response to this form of social organization and functioned with that form of organization to promote maximum efficiency in the production and accumulation of surplus (Karp and Kelly, 1971b).

During the early rise of the market system for the production and consumption of wealth, ideologies developed that justified the emerging market institution. The Protestant Ethic, with its emphasis on hard work, is well known. A job became seen as a sacred calling, and success at work was evidence that a man had been chosen for salvation. The main source of a man's identity was in the job he held; his status was allocated accordingly. Along with this emphasis on work, there developed an emphasis on rationality or "the methodical attainment of a definitely given and practical end by means of an increasingly precise calculation of adequate means." The notion of work as the main source of identity, the idea of economic success as a measure of salvation, and rationalism—all are consistent with the rise of capitalistic activity.

Capitalistic activity has been defined by Weber as follows:

We will define a capitalistic economic action as one which rests on the expectation of profit by the utilization of opportunities for exchange, that is on (formally) peaceful chances of profit. Acquisition by force (formally and actually) follows its own particular laws, and it is not expedient, however little one can forbid this, to place it in the same category with action which is, in the last analysis, oriented to profits from exchange. Where capitalistic acquisition is rationally pursued, the corresponding action is adjusted to calculations in terms of capital. This means that the action is adapted to a systematic utilization of goods or personal services as means of acquisition in such a way that, at the close of a business period, the balance of the enterprise in money assets (or, in estimated money value of assets) exceeds the capital, i.e., the estimated value of the material means of production used for acquisition in exchange. [Weber, 1958, p. 17–18]

Given this definition of capitalistic activity, Weber hypothesized that such activity results from the actor's orientation to a particular set of values, which he defined as the "spirit" or ethic of capitalism. The salient characteristic of this ethic is the motivational commitment to the unlimited acquisition of profit as an end in itself.

In fact, the *summum bonum* of this ethic, the earning of more and more money, combined with the strict avoidance of all spontaneous enjoyment of life, is above all completely devoid of any eudaemon-

istic, not to say hedonistic, admixture. It is thought of so purely as
an end in itself, that from the point of view of the happiness of, or
utility to, the single individual, it appears entirely transcendental
and absolutely irrational. Man is dominated by the making of
money, by acquisition as the ultimate purpose of his life. Economic
acquisition is no longer subordinated to man as the means for the
satisfaction of his material needs. [Weber, 1958, p. 53]

This, of course, touches on an important point: through the
development of capitalism and the "spirit" that goes with it,
man began his move toward a vast increase in his ability to
produce economic goods. However, in the process, economic
acquisition, economic growth, and increased production became
ends in themselves, rather than means toward the end of satisfying physical needs and allowing men to satisfy their self
needs.

However, the emergence of capitalistic activity and its corresponding *Weltanschauung* set the stage for the massive increase
in production of economic goods which occurred during the Industrial Revolution.

Industrialism was not superimposed directly upon the feudal social
system of the Middle Ages but was preceded by a series of gradual
changes which laid the foundation for its development. Probably
the most important of these changes was the commercial revolution
of the sixteenth and seventeenth centuries, which resulted in active
world markets for goods produced by industry in the next century.
Techniques of production, however, had changed little, at least by
comparison with the technological developments accompanying the
Industrial Revolution, between the eighteenth century and the time
man first discovered how to use tools. The social organization of
production had also changed very little during this whole period.
At the time the Industrial Revolution began, the family was still the
basic production unit. This was clearly true of agricultural production, in which the vast majority of people were engaged. The manufacturing that occurred was also done predominantly in individual
households under the domestic system. Raw materials were either
bought by the workers or provided by a middleman, and the products were manufactured in the home and were then sold either di-

rectly to customers or to dealers who marketed them. [Faunce, 1968, p. 15]

About the middle of the eighteenth century in England, the application of rationality and science to the end of improving production techniques produced a series of inventions that transformed the world as never before.

The specific inventions that were most instrumental in starting the industrialization process were the flying shuttle (1733), the coking of coal (1735), the use of coke in blast furnaces (1740), the spinning jenny (1767), the water frame (1769), the steam engine (1769), the spinning mule (1779), the "puddling" process of making steel (1784), the power loom (1787), and the cotton gin (1792). There is a historical relationship between these inventions in the sense that each occurred in response to a particular need at a specific point in the process of technological development. The process was set in motion with the invention of more efficient looms. Cotton thread could not be produced fast enough to supply these looms, and new spinning equipment was developed. Further development of spinning and weaving machinery was limited by the use of human power, and the use first of the water wheel and then of the steam engine can be seen as a response to this need. The increasing necessity for metal in the manufacture of production machinery might have slowed the whole process of development had it not been for improvements in the manufacture of iron. Prior to the eighteenth century, smelting and all preparation of iron were done with charcoal, and the virtual deforestation of England was the result. The discovery of the way to make coke from coal and the use of coke in blast-furnace operation provided a major impetus to the growth of the English iron and steel industries. The enormous growth of the textile industry stimulated development in other industries as well. Increased output and the resulting necessity for broader markets provided an added incentive for improvement in transportation and communication. Developments in mining, agricultural technology, and in the processing of raw materials, for example, the invention of the cotton gin, were spurred by the greater need for raw materials growing out of improved production techniques. The technological developments in the textile industry thus ramified throughout the whole economy of England and, eventually, of the world. [Faunce, 1968, pp. 16–17]

The increased ability to use energy that resulted from the mechanization of production, allowed an increase in production well beyond anything that had existed in any past era. The non-human factor in production—machines—became increasingly important. However, the institutions allowing for the right to consume this increased production, recognized only the right to consume through the human factor—labor—for most of the population.

The heavy emphasis on the value of work as an end in itself, and the fact that in industrial societies a man's source of identity is in his occupation, meant that in order to have any meaningful status at all in such societies, a man must work. It was thus necessary to have full employment so that every man would have some chance to develop a meaningful identity, and also because the alternative to working, in many cases, was starvation.

The ownership of the nonhuman factor, capital, became more and more concentrated instead of becoming spread throughout the population. The result was an imbalance between production and consumption. Production was increasingly affected by machines while the right to consume was still, for the vast majority, based on labor (Kelso and Adler, 1958, p. 93). Those few who had the right to consume through ownership of the nonhuman factor could not possibly use all of the wealth that could be produced by an industrial economy. The bulk of the population, which still suffered scarcity of consumer goods, could have consumed the wealth that machine production made possible, but there was no institutional arrangement to allow them to do so. The one-factor distribution-system that evolved before industrial societies, remained in force even though there were two factors operating in the productive system. This basic imbalance made it increasingly difficult for societies in the early stages of industrial capitalism to consume their own product.

Spotting this basic weakness in industrial capitalism, Marx

predicted that it would eventually collapse. Whether we would have been better or worse off if it had collapsed, is a moot point, but it didn't, because men found ways to patch up the system without correcting its basic flaws. Two different patchwork systems evolved from early primitive capitalism.

One system, practiced by the Soviet Union since the 1917 revolution, involves state ownership of the nonhuman factor of production. Since the state owns this productive factor, it also is able to consume the product of this production. This maintains a balance between production and consumption, and avoids recession, depression, and other results of an unbalanced system. However, as far as the individual human beings in such a system are concerned, their right to consume still is determined by the single factor of labor. The state owns all, the productive process rolls on, but the human beings involved have become trapped as slaves of the state. Although those who built this system call it socialism, it can best be referred to as "state capitalism," since the state, run by a few bureaucrats, is the only capitalist and the people are all laborers.

The other offspring of primitive capitalism that developed in the so-called western democracies is, of course, the welfare state, here referred to as "mixed capitalism." This system, which flowered after the near collapse of the whole game during the Great Depression, rests upon the assumption of the ideology of Keynesian economics.

This ideology recognizes that industrial economies will face the problem of supply exceeding demand. Demand is thus created by a series of clever devices such as labor unions (which get higher wages for workers, thus increasing their purchasing power), the welfare system (which provides small amounts of money for those who are unable to work if they are willing to have their lives controlled in return and which also creates jobs for many welfare functionaries), government employment programs (this is called "creating jobs"), and biggest and best of all, government spending to keep demand high. The only problem with the government-spending part is that the government is unable to spend enough on human needs (due to a complicated ideology which holds that human beings should satisfy their own needs through toil) and therefore, spends primarily to build huge defense establishments and great military machines. Enemies are then invented for the military machines to fight, since they must of course exist for some reason. Under the welfare state, a large proportion of the population eventually reaches a fair degree of affluence despite the creakiness of the patchwork system. However, a good-sized proportion of the population continues to live in poverty in the midst of plenty.

Within the welfare states, great arguments range between the classical (conservative) economists and the Keynesian (liberal) economists. The conservatives claim that if the government would quit meddling in the economy, the invisible hand of the free market would lead to a balanced economy and full employment. The liberals argue that increasing demand through government spending and high wages for workers, will balance the economy and give us full employment. Meanwhile, the proponents of state capitalism argue that only government ownership of the means of production will bring prosperity and full employment. Great heated arguments take place between disciples of these three approaches on how best to accomplish the desired ends. Like many arguments that take place within a given social reality, however, these arguments never do get to the root of the problem, since they never raise questions about the underlying assumptions upon which all present industrial societies rest.

Here we come to another underlying assumption that needs to be examined. Conservatives, liberals, and government-ownership buffs all agree that a major goal of the economic system is full employment. This goal is accepted only because everyone accepts the assumption that the only way for the bulk of the population to consume the wealth that is produced is to gain access to distribution through the one factor of labor (Kelso and Hetter, 1969). Under state capitalism there is no choice, since only the state can consume through ownership of the non-human productive factor. In the welfare states, only a small proportion of the population can consume through ownership of the nonhuman factor. For instance, only about 10 percent of American families own corporate stocks, and less than 1 percent of American families receive at least half of the annual income they spend on consumption in the form of return on invested capital (Kelso and Hetter, 1969, pp. 40–46).

Thus, despite the existence of highly industrialized economies that produce through two factors, only through one factor —labor—are most people allowed to consume. Despite the government's "creation" of jobs (an ironic term which suggests the absurdity of the whole operation), despite featherbedding's establishment of numerous useless jobs, many are still unemployed and poverty still exists. Meanwhile, the state continues to build bigger armaments, and advertisers attempt to create needs in order to keep aggregate demand high. It seems unbelievable that no one would start dealing with the root of the problem, but everyone is too busy fighting false battles about the best way to maintain full employment.

Thus, our modern technologies have produced several huge work-states in which nearly everyone continues to toil desperately to make ends meet, where loss of jobs to automation is considered a threat, and where blacks and whites battle over who shall have the honor to toil for the corporations. Anyone who suggests that persons be allowed to share in the distribution of wealth through a second factor other than his labor is looked upon as a crazy utopian dreamer who is out of touch with reality. As with all social realities, the current one is viewed as the only one, and you'd better keep in touch with it or you are obviously some sort of nut.

We see here, then, the strange situation in which man's material creations (technology) might have been used to satisfy his basic needs and allow humans to concentrate on their self needs. But man's nonmaterial creations (institutions) have prevented this, since a laboristic distribution of production has become reified to such an extent that men have become trapped in the webs of their own creations. The large industrial work-states that result do not even succeed in satisfying basic needs, let alone self needs. Human freedom is practically nonexistent, since nearly everyone must work for someone else (either the corporation or the state).

Yet most citizens of the welfare states consider themselves to be free people living in democratic societies. Also, it is unlikely that Soviet citizens see themselves as slaves of the state. Whether people see themselves as free or not depends mainly on how they define the word "free." Soviet citizens are free to find the best position that they can within the confines of their system. Likewise, Americans are free to choose for which corporation they will toil and are free to rise within the confines of their system. What, then, do I mean by a "free" or "democratic" society, and what is the difference, if any, between Soviet and American societies in this respect? For surely, we are free and they are not.

Essentially, I would see a full democracy as one in which every citizen had both economic and political freedom. In an agrarian society, economic freedom meant owning your own land (the nonhuman factor) so that your labor would be your own. In an industrial society it would mean ownership of the right to consume the production of the nonhuman factor, which would be spread throughout the population instead of being the exclusive right of 1 per cent of the population or of the state. (Ways of achieving this will be discussed later.) It should be apparent that this is different from the right to choose for whom you work or the right to invest in a small business and go broke. These are rather hollow economic freedoms. Political freedom refers to what we usually think of when we use that term: the right to vote, freedom of speech, and other such rights (the sorts of things guaranteed by the American Constitution but often not allowed in practice). It is generally stated that political democracy requires a literate population with a fairly high degree of what we now call education. This is true—such things are necessary for partial political democracy. A fully operating political democracy would require a population that had received an education that had provided them with "built-in shockproof crap detectors" (Postman and Weingartner, 1969). This will be discussed again later.

Using these criteria, then, what sort of freedom exists in the industrialized states of the current era? Since the Soviet Union provides neither economic nor political freedom, it is, as everyone but the population of that state knows, a totalitarian state. The United States, which is similar to other western nations, provides the rather hollow form of economic freedom of which conservatives are so proud and the partial political freedom of which liberals are so proud. The United States (and similar countries) can best be referred to as a semidemocracy. I think it is important to make these distinctions between totalitarian, semidemocratic, and democratic states. If you try to point out to an American that he does not live in a free society, he will point to the Soviet Union, mention that we are obviously freer than they are, and tell you to go live there if you don't like it here. Also, some radicals, in attempting to show persons what is wrong with the United States, fail to distinguish between totalitarian and semidemocratic states. Given a choice, most persons would choose the latter, but that does not mean that the latter is a free society. A semidemocracy does allow you to complain vigorously (as I am doing here), and this is something, although one could make a good case that the reason we are allowed to complain is because no one will listen to us.

What it gets down to, then, is that we currently have a choice between totalitarian work-states and semidemocratic work-states. Because of machine technology, both types provide reasonable satisfaction of the basic needs for some of the people. Neither allows satisfaction of the self needs. It appears that you can fool most of the people all of the time.

The emergence of capitalism, when combined with the Industrial Revolution to create our present system of industrial capitalism, brought about a massive increase in the ability of human beings to produce economic goods (goods needed to satisfy the physical needs of human beings). This development, in many ways, had the potential to solve the problem that had determined the activity of most human beings up to that development—the scarcity of economic goods.

However, the spirit of capitalism—and indeed, the spirit of industrialism—emphasized and legitimized activity aimed at producing surplus, making profits, and expanding endlessly the production of economic goods. The entire social organization of industrial societies came to rest on the assumptions of increased production as an end in itself, full employment as an end in itself, a man's identity as rooted in his job or occupation, and overall, the main goal of social organization and human activity as an increase in the Gross National Product.

This meant that those aspects of the human potential best suited to increased production became the accepted and highest-ranking aspects, which were incorporated into the social straw man, which became the model of social acceptance. Those aspects of the human potential that might interfere with increased production (the hedonistic, erotic, expressive, empathic, and idealistic aspects) were denied or given a lower status.

The distribution of the right to consume through the single means of jobholding, ensured that this would be the main source of a man's identity and also ensured that few people would be freed from the need to toil. The attachment of the words "freedom" and "democracy" to the resulting situation ensured that few persons would look for any greater freedom, for how can one seek freedom if one is already free?

All industrial states currently utilize a laboristic system of distribution despite their production systems' heavy reliance on the nonhuman factor. A laboristic distribution system requires labor, whether or not it is needed for production of wealth

(Kelso and Hetter, 1969). Industrial societies must turn all activities into labor regardless of whether those activities have anything to do with the production of consumer goods. It is the process by which this is accomplished to which I will turn next, as we try to get to the heart of the sickness of industrial societies, which leads to its rejection by many of the young.

FOUR

Driven Man: Alienation in Industrial Society

In the attempt to provide for basic human needs, men engage in activities that can be classified as labor. This would include toil (heavy physical work) and all things which are necessary for the production of economic goods. The self needs, on the other hand, would require activities of the type known as leisure. By leisure, I do not mean free time or time not spent working. Rather, I am referring to leisure as the ancient Greeks saw it.

In this sense, leisure is a state of being in which activity is performed for its own sake or as its own end. Leisure activities are those that are desirable in themselves and are never performed for the sake of anything else. Essentially, leisure is freedom from the necessity of being occupied with activities that are done for extrinsic reasons. In its narrowest sense, leisure refers to contemplation and the playing of music. In a broader sense, it would include philosophy, art, pure science, poetry, social intercourse with friends chosen for their own worth, and similar activities. In an even broader conception, almost any activity, including strenuous physical work, could be leisure activity if it is performed for its own sake. Likewise, even the playing of music can become labor work if it is done to obtain some external reward.

When societies are in a state of economic scarcity, most activities are performed for extrinsic reasons. A set of extrinsic rewards must be distributed in such a way as to ensure that those activities necessary for the survival of society are performed (Davis and Moore, 1945). Societies have available rewards aimed at basic needs (those which provide sustenance and comfort) and rewards aimed at self needs (those which provide self respect and ego expansion).

In the complex societies, especially industrial societies, stratification is the device by which such societies ensure that the most important activities are performed by qualified persons (or, at least, by persons who appear to be qualified). Through a differential distribution of rewards whereby persons performing those activities functionally of greatest importance to the society receive the greater rewards, societies see that less important activities do not compete successfully with more essential ones (Davis and Moore, 1945). Those activities are most essential that provide subsistence goods.

From the beginning of civilization, life is fragmented. The industrial era greatly increases this fragmentation as mechanical technology leads to increasing division of labor, with tasks split up into parts for greater efficiency and increased production. Roles (expectations for behavior) are attached to each specialized pattern of activity. These direct the person performing that activity as to how the activity will be performed.

The fragmented roles are integrated through the institutional arrangement known as bureaucracy. Bureaucracy is the predominant form of social organization in industrial societies, extending to all organized patterns of activity, be they industrial, governmental, educational, military, religious, voluntary, or whatever. Bureaucracies are characterized by a well-defined chain of command structured on the lines of a pyramid, a system of procedures and rules for dealing with all contingencies relating to the activities involved, a division of labor based on specialization, promotion and selection based on technical competence (meritocracy), and impersonality in human relations (Bennis and Slater, 1963, p. 53).

Under this form of institutional arrangement, activities are performed according to rather exacting, pre-existing institutional patterns. Since tasks are fragmented and reified institutions are alienating, extrinsic rewards play an important role in getting persons to perform the necessary tasks. These rewards are distributed differentially through the mechanism of jobholding, since this is the only mode of distribution which exists for most persons.

Since relationships between persons in a bureaucratic organization are impersonal or role relations, each person projects a public self to maintain the image that he is what the role requires him to be. Since each person only sees the public self of each of the others, the universal fake-out results. This has the function of keeping the hierarchical authority arrangements and differential distribution of rewards intact. If it were not for the secrecy and image making of those on a given level, there is always the possibility that someone on a lower level might discover that the emperor wore no clothes.

Bureaucracies are especially efficient for the organization of repetitive activities in an unchanging environment. They were especially suited to the values and demands of the Victorian era (Bennis and Slater, 1963, p. 53). They have nearly always been recognized as a hindrance to open human interaction, and there is some question whether they are efficient in a rapidly changing modern society (more on this later).

As industrialization proceeds, automation and economic surplus allow more persons to move from primary pursuits (agriculture) to secondary pursuits (industry) to tertiary pursuits (service occupations). In the United States, less than 5 percent of the population is engaged in agriculture, and a decreasing percentage is engaged in industry. Service occupations now show the largest increases.

Increasing economic surplus also allows more people to engage in intrinsically interesting activities—art, philosophy, music, pure science, conversation, teaching, learning, etc. These we could refer to as quadrary or fourth-level activities: those which are done for their own sake and are rather far removed from basic resource extraction and the production of economic goods. That is, with increasing automation and economic surplus, we begin to reach a stage in which the possibility of engaging in leisure activities increases. But as we look around us, we do not see many activities that are performed for their own sake. People are teaching, learning, philosophizing, making music, and so forth, but they are doing these things for extrinsic reasons as jobs.

In an economic system that distributes wealth only on the basis of one factor—labor—all activities become transformed into labor through their performance as jobs. Intrinsically interesting activities are done for extrinsic rewards, and their character is thereby changed.

Our educational institutions provide a good example of this. First, they are organized on the model of the industrial factory with the learning experience fragmented into courses, subjects, and the like, which are "learned" at preset times in forty-minute or fifty-minute periods. In addition, the main purpose of the educational system is to prepare people for jobs, both by giving them skills which will be useful on the job, and perhaps even more important, getting them used to being on time, working during preset periods of time, and engaging in activity for the sake of earning external rewards. During this process, learning, an intrinsically interesting activity, becomes transformed into a boring task done for grades, gold stars, and other extrinsic rewards. The devastating results of this are well documented (Robertson and Steele, 1971).

Knowledge-seeking, which certainly is an intrinsically interesting activity, is done in academic departments in universities as part of a job. A series of rewards (monetary, promotions, tenure) are offered to ensure that people are motivated to seek knowledge. Departments worry about their national ranking (another extrinsic reward), and despair sets in if the "production" of a department fails.

As I noted before, the reified institution of distributing

wealth through labor requires labor. Jobs will either be invented to keep people busy, or activities which might well be done for other reasons will be transformed into jobs. A justifying ideology, which consists in large part of the "explanations" of economics and sociology, lends credence to this process by discussing the "functional necessity" of activities and the "inputs" and "outputs" that are attached to these.

As a society moves from economic scarcity to the ability to provide a decent standard of living for all its members, one might expect that extrinsic rewards that provide sustenance and comfort would no longer be effective as motivators. However, a one-factor distribution-system ensures that even as affluence sets in, the threat of starvation is always handy to keep people going. Even then, we might expect that people would work to satisfy their basic needs and then seek to fulfill their self needs through leisure activities.

However, we noted earlier that the institutional arrangements in industrial societies that result in the universal fake-out do not allow persons to develop an accurate and acceptable self-concept. Instead persons misdirect their energies and seek indirect self-acceptance through seeking prestige, status, and status-oriented consumption beyond the level needed to live comfortably. Thus, the society has an additional set of extrinsic rewards available to motivate people. And since it is not possible to develop an accurate and acceptable self-concept through indirect means, the unfulfilled need becomes the driving force that keeps industrial societies running. Unfortunately, they run for their own sake rather than for any humanistic reasons.

Thus we come full circle in our analysis of industrial societies. Above and beyond the subsistence level where perhaps they were necessary, activities are done for extrinsic rewards through jobholding, and the value of the rewards depends upon unfulfilled need for self-acceptance. Further, the excess consumption that then results helps, under the Keynesian model of the economy, to ensure full employment (which, of course, is seen as an end in itself). Full employment keeps everyone busy (thus preventing leisure) and also provides funds for additional consumption in the quest for indirect self-acceptance. And so, round and round we go on the merry-go-round. The entire system that human beings have created (technology and institutions) becomes reified and confronts men as something which exists outside themselves. A vast, dehumanized world is created in which man's own creations dominate him.

We noted earlier that one of the basic self needs of human beings is the need to expand the self through action. To satisfy this need, men must have control over their own activities and must act as conscious, creative human beings. By externalizing themselves through activity, human beings create both technology and institutions. Through the processes of objectification and reification (which I discussed earlier), humans come to experience their own creations as something apart from themselves and become alienated from them. As Marx noted, man's labor becomes alienated in that it is experienced as something controlled by forces outside himself.

Alienation (or "estrangement") means, for Marx, that man does *not* experience himself as the acting agent in his grasp of the world, but that the world (nature, others, and he himself) remain alien to him. They stand above and against him as objects, even though they may be objects of his own creation. Alienation is essentially experiencing the world and oneself passively, receptively, as the subject separated from the object. [Fromm, 1961, p. 44]

When activities are performed for extrinsic rewards, they are controlled by those who distribute the rewards rather than by those who are engaged in the activities. Further, in most occupational activities, one must not only correctly perform the assigned tasks but also properly act out the social role that goes with the position he occupies. This involves projecting a public self or self-image that fits the behavioral expectations of the social role. Since these expectations are largely determined by those who control the rewards given for proper performance of the role, they are likely not to represent what the performer actually is. That is, the person playing the role must hide those aspects of his self that are not proper in that role. This always requires a certain amount of effort and creates a certain amount of dissonance in the person playing the role. This dissonance can be reduced if the person playing the role by projecting a public self comes to believe that his social role is what he actually is. He can do this by repressing (becoming unaware of) those aspects of his self which do not fit his social role. He is then acting the role in bad faith and becomes alienated from parts of his self in the way I discussed earlier. The person who performs a role in bad faith—that is, comes to believe that he *is* that social role—will probably give the most convincing performance since he is, indeed, committed to that role. In this case, the person derives his self-esteem from the performance of the activities appropriate to his occupational role and thus does not feel alienated from his job. However, obtaining indirect self-acceptance in this manner, leads him to become alienated from parts of his self. On the other hand, the person who does not believe he is the social role he is performing, is less likely to be alienated from his self but may very well feel alienated from the activity he has to perform in his occupational role.

This is a rather complicated matter, for in a sense it involves two kinds of alienation, although the two types can only be separated conceptually since they actually are interrelated. Perhaps it would be helpful to look at the four possible combinations of the two types of alienation in order to shed some light on how they are related.

In an ideal or utopian situation, men would engage in intrinsically interesting activity and would derive self-esteem from this because they would be meeting the need to expand the self through action. The activity in which they were engaging would be free activity in the sense that it would not be performed for any extrinsic monetary reward or to gain indirect self-acceptance by trying to elicit a positive response to a public self. This could only happen in a situation in which the people involved provided social support for direct self-acceptance by accepting each other in a way that allowed each person to reveal all that he was without fear of rejection. This type of situation could theoretically exist in modern societies in situations related neither to the economic sphere nor to performance of occupational duties. It is unlikely that such situations occur very often, however, since most people derive their ways of interacting from their occupational roles and carry these over even into situations that do not require them. Since nearly all occupations are tied directly to extrinsic rewards through the process of earning a living, the activities associated with them become labor work, and it is also usually necessary to interact on the basis of the universal fake-out. Consequently, the utopian situation in which men experience neither alienated activity nor self-alienation, rarely occurs in modern industrial societies. Instead, one of three other situations usually occurs.

For most persons in industrial societies, the activity in which they engage as a job is not a prime source of self-esteem, and they are consequently indifferent to their work activities, not committed to them, and somewhat alienated from them. At the same time, their daily interaction with other human beings is mainly in the context of situations that require the projection of a public self-image, and this sort of interaction is carried over into other situations. Thus, for most persons in industrial societies, especially those of low occupational status, both alienated activity and self-alienation exist.

For some persons in higher-status occupations, especially the professions, occupational activities are more directly linked to the person's self-esteem, and in that sense these persons are not alienated from their activities but are, rather, committed to the occupational roles (Faunce, 1968, pp. 124–127). However, since adequate performance of these roles involves pleasing those who control the rewards associated with them (increased salary, promotions, and the like), these persons are likely to go through the process of dissonance reduction which I described earlier, play their roles in bad faith, and not be able to develop an accurate and acceptable self-concept, since they are unable to obtain direct self-acceptance. That is, persons in this situation attempt to gain self-acceptance indirectly through their careers. What this involves has been nicely summed up by Slater in his discussion of whether women suffer in American society because they have been deprived of careers:

Many people would object that most women don't *want* careers. I suspect the women themselves would agree, but I also wonder if deep inside they don't feel the kind of puzzled uneasiness that we always experience when obliged to accept a formulation that makes us lose either way. The problem is that "career" is in itself a masculine concept (i.e., designed for males in our society). When we say "career" it connotes a demanding, rigorous, preordained life pattern, to whose goals everything else is ruthlessly subordinated—everything pleasurable, human, emotional, bodily, frivolous. It is a stern, Calvinistic word, which is why it always has a humorous effect when it is applied to occupational patterns of a less puritanical sort. Thus when a man asks a woman if she wants a career, it is intimidating. He is saying, are you willing to suppress half of your being as I am, neglect your family as I do, exploit personal relationships as I do, renounce all personal spontaneity as I do? Naturally, she shudders a bit and shuffles back to the broom closet. [Slater, 1970, p. 72]

This characteristic of professional careers as they exist in modern societies was summed up by a professional, who, in an unguarded moment, noted that "a professional should be a driven man." This is fine if the person has convinced himself that it is the nature of human beings to be driven men. For those who do not accept that idea, another response is possible in modern societies, and it too alleviates one form of alienation while the other still exists. The difference is that the other response involves trading self-alienation for alienated activity.

For persons who do not play their social roles in bad faith, it is less likely that their major source of self-esteem will come from a convincing performance of those roles. These people may enjoy the activity in which they engage in their occupations and even perform it quite well. However, the convincing role-performance or "image" is likely to be missing. Their major source of self-esteem is likely to be sought through obtaining direct self-acceptance from groups of close friends. As a consequence, they are not as likely to be committed to the performance of their occupational roles to the extent that the career-oriented are. To the extent that they are able to gain direct self-acceptance, these people may be able to overcome the self-alienation that characterizes modern societies, but they are likely to be more acutely aware of the alienated activity that they are performing. That is, they are likely to feel that the activity they engage in is controlled by those who dispense rewards to such an extent that it is not really free activity at all. Since in modern societies most activities have been transformed into labor work, it is difficult to avoid this feeling of alienation.

It seems then that modern industrial societies are characterized by three types of situations. Most people in these societies find themselves in situations in which they experience both self-alienation and alienated activity. A smaller number of people who are engaged in relatively high-status careers may avoid the feeling of alienated activity but still experience self-alienation. A still smaller number may overcome the general self-alienation but still experience a feeling of alienated activity. In a sense, modern societies are populated by the alienated, the committed, and the outsiders; none of these is fully able to satisfy their self needs. Of course, we must keep in mind that these categories are only conceptual devices and that it is unlikely that people can actually be divided up into these types, but I do think that this typology helps to clarify the problem of alienation in industrial societies. What is important, however, is not so much the different psychological reactions, but, rather, the sociological process by which activity becomes alienated under industrial capitalism.

Thus, we are faced with a situation in which the technological progress of modern industrial societies has brought about a situation in which it is possible to satisfy the physical needs of the population but in which there is also an increased deprivation of the self needs. Before the Industrial Revolution, most people experienced life as peasants in a village economy. Within the traditional values of the village, developing a self-image was not particularly difficult. Since there was only one version of social reality, this reality had a solid objective appearance. There did not exist competing realities to render it transparent. Who a person was, was largely determined by his sex and the family into which he had been born. A traditional pattern comprised the core of a person's self-image, which could be taken for granted. The peasant was unable to conceive of being anything other than what he was, and this had been determined by the position into which he was born, which was accepted as an act of God. In a real sense, the question "Who am I?" simply did not arise.

There are advantages in terms of contentment in not being torn by questions of identity. However, the peasant gained these advantages through not being aware of alternative conceptions of what he might be, and indeed, not being aware of the possibility of alternative realities.

Yet the roots which nurtured the peasant also bound him. The very factors which facilitated the satisfaction of his self needs made it difficult for him to transcend the limitations of his culture. His unquestioned acceptance of a traditional self-image was matched by the fatalism with which he regarded poverty and serfdom. Such choices as he made were unencumbered by confusion about himself, but this lack of confusion was largely a reflection of his lack of self-awareness. [Putney and Putney, 1964, p. 179]

The Industrial Revolution brought about a massive increase in the ability to produce consumer goods and to satisfy the physical needs. The division of labor and consequent development of competing social realities, as different segments of the population lived in different social worlds, brought about an increased self-awareness and an increased ability to make choices about his identity.

Thus the American—indeed, the member of any industrial society —has an intense awareness of self such as his peasant ancestors never experienced. He has, therefore, a greater need to understand and to accept himself. As industrialization has led to a gradually rising standard of living, the physical needs have become less compelling and the self needs have assumed greater relative importance in human motivation. They have also assumed a greater absolute importance, for as men have achieved heightened self-awareness their need for self-acceptance has become proportionally stronger.

The American's need to develop an accurate and acceptable self-image is intense, but his opportunities for fulfilling this need are unparalleled. He has a broad range of meaningful activity open to him and unlimited opportunity for warm and candid association with disparate individuals. He has the opportunity to exist as a conscious, articulated self to a degree seldom before realized in man's history. Adrift in an industrial society, the American is forced to choose—free to choose—and acutely aware of the self which chooses. He has an ideal situation for achieving autonomy, for being able to choose himself and his behavior in the light of his needs.

Yet it is a rare American who does achieve autonomy. Most still cling to modes of behavior which may have been functional in an earlier social order, but which are now only misdirected and neurotic patterns. Time and technology have vitiated the traditional means of achieving self-acceptance. [Putney and Putney, 1964, pp. 183–184]

As I indicated above, the technology and institutions that human beings have created confront them as something that exists outside themselves. The result is that with the opportunity to fulfill his self needs, modern man seems incapable of doing so.

However, despite the complaints of a few intellectuals (who, after all, are out of touch with reality) there is no great concern about this. To be concerned about something, one first has to be aware of it; the universal fake-out plus the mystifications of social scientists and others prevent most people from identifying the root of the unease which grips industrial societies.

After all, advanced technology ensures that most people are well-fed and comfortable (we do have some poverty in the midst of plenty, but this gives everyone something to worry about—like how to create jobs for the poor). The workers, who were supposed to rebel against a system that alienates their activity, instead pushed for higher wages and were absorbed. Dissent is allowed in a semidemocracy and most protest is absorbed. It would not appear that much would disturb such a one-dimensional society.

Now it is true that some of the population (blacks, Chicanos, etc.) never was absorbed into the jobholding economic system, and they started raising hell. But, of course, if we can only provide good jobs for them, they too will fit in.

However, modern industrial societies support large educational institutions. Over a period of time, a large number of people are situated in these institutions, and it is the educated who are most likely to be aware of alienation and the most likely to see it as a problem. In the decade of the 1960s, a great deal of unrest and turmoil occurred among the affluent young, and to this we now turn.

FIVE

The Obsolete Generation: Youth in Industrial Society

A social reality, culture, or worldview is created through the interaction of conscious, striving human beings as they attempt to make sense of the world in which they live. A common social reality will be shared by those persons whose social situation is similar and who are engaged in similar activities. As a culture develops among those who are interacting in a common activity, ideologies will arise to justify and explain the patterns of behavior practiced by those who share that culture.

This suggests that a social movement or counter-culture movement can only arise in a society if there is some collectivity that shares a social situation different from that of those who create and maintain the mainstream culture of that society. There must be a group of human beings whose shared activities are not legitimited and justified by the existing ideological system. They must experience a sense of discomfort as a result of the disjunction between their situation and the existing societal goals, and begin to perceive the existing values and goals as problematic. Under such conditions, it is likely that a new social reality will begin to emerge, deriving its character from the ecological situation of those human beings who are creating it.

In this chapter I will attempt to show how technological changes in mature industrial societies have produced a group whose social situation and activities are not supported by the prevailing ideology which provides social status and acceptance for persons on the basis of their occupational niches and stresses the importance of what a person does, in an occupational sense, as a major portion of his identity. It is the thesis here that increased automation has removed a portion of our population from the labor force for such a long period of time that the basic ethic of industrial capitalism, which derives from a person's position in that labor force, no longer has any meaning to that "class" in our society.

In addition, rapid technological change brings about changes in the structure of the family, so that the young are able to develop new ways of looking at the world based upon their immediate experience rather than on the social reality passed to them by the preceding generation.

A particular version of social reality is generally passed from generation to generation through the process of socialization. The family is one of the most important socializing institutions in a society. When the environment is relatively stable and unchanging, the experiences of the parents will be viable role-models for children, as the future is likely to be similar to the past. The family will likely be authoritarian in order effectively to pass the experiences of one generation on to the next. Since the activities and social situation of a generation are similar to those of the preceding one, the existing reality provides a meaningful interpretation of the world.

If the environment is changing, however, it is likely that the past experiences of parents will not provide a viable example for children, since the future may be quite different from the past. Under conditions of rapid change, the family is likely to be more democratic. Social distance between parents and children is small, parental authority is relatively mild, and the child is not seen as a mere parental possession without an independent legal status. The democratic family is more efficient under conditions of rapid social change, since children must be relatively free to adapt to new conditions and not be hindered by traditional ways of doing things (Bennis and Slater, 1963, p. 20).

Rapid social change creates an experiential chasm between parents and their children. The world that the parents experienced no longer exists, and the parents have no experience relevant to the world in which the children exist (Bennis and Slater, 1963, p. 20). Under these conditions, susceptibility to the immediate social environment is increased for children. The value-system of the parents does not provide a meaningful justification for the activities in which the children are engaging. Since their common situation is different from that of their parents, the young will begin to create a new social reality through interaction with their peers. This will be especially so if persons of the same general age are removed from the family situation and there are institutions in the society which engage them on an age-graded basis. This is likely to be the case in universalistic societies. Rapid social change, then, creates the conditions for the much-discussed generation gap.

In the United States, almost from the founding of the nation, there have been a number of factors that favored the democratic family over the authoritarian family and produced an experiential chasm between parents and their children (Bennis and Slater, 1963, p. 31). The early settlers were transplanted from Europe and did not have experience with the new world in which their children were growing up. The settling of the West continued the experiential gap between parents and children, as parents were not used to the new territories in which their children were raised. After the settling of the West, the great immigration of the latter nineteenth century brought forth parents who were unaccustomed to the styles of life in their adopted nation, while their children were growing up in that nation and adapting to it faster. All of these factors produced a tradition of a democratic family in the United States.

The most recent, and probably most important, environmen-

tal change that produced an experiential gap between generations, is rapid technological change. The shift from an agricultural society to an early stage of industrialization, the shift from
early industrialization to a more mature industrial society, and,
most recently, the movement into a postindustrial society, have
all left chasms between generations.

Of these, the most recent gap between the parents of the Depression experience and their offspring of the affluent postmod-
ern society has been the greatest. The rate of technological
change has increased greatly, and this increases the likelihood
that the experiences of parents will not be relevant to their children. In addition, in the last thirty years, American society has
begun the shift from scarcity to abundance. This is one of the
most drastic shifts in the history of man, since all of past experience has been characterized by scarcity for the bulk of the
population. All of the traditions, institutions, values, and the
like, of past generations have been shaped by the scarcity of
goods to satisfy the basic needs. The relevance of these will be
somewhat tenuous to the first generation raised under conditions of somewhat general affluence.

Probably the values most affected by the affluent society are
those toward work and deferred gratification. Under conditions
of scarcity, and especially during the early stages of industrialization, it was necessary that every man work; in order to get
ahead, deferred gratification was crucial. The Protestant Ethic
supports such values as hard work, thrift, putting off pleasure,
etc.

As automation of industry proceeds, however, increased production begins to undermine the scarcity-based ethic of deferred gratification (Cohen, 1967, pp. 203–207). Also, the decreasing need for labor allows the development of a stage of
adolescence between the childhood period and the time a person takes an adult role as a worker in the economic system.
Adolescence is a relatively new development in human societies, in which a young person, past the age of puberty, remains

a special sort of child with no function except to go to school. The emphasis on universal schooling for practically all those in a particular age-group places the young in a situation where a good deal of their activity is performed through interaction with their age peers. If there are common problems shared by the young as a result of their position in advanced industrial societies, we would expect a youth culture to emerge in response to these problems.

When we look at the situation of the young in industrial societies, we find ourselves explaining their changing position in the society in terms of their relationship to the economic system. In the early stages of industrialization, when labor was needed, children worked in factories at an early age. Even as the need for child labor decreased, there were still unskilled and semiskilled jobs which the young could fill. However, increasing automation began to remove the need for unskilled and semiskilled labor and made it desirable to keep the young out of the labor market so that they would not compete with adults for the remaining unskilled and semiskilled jobs.

With increasing automation, a period of limbo develops between childhood and adult status. Between the ages of about twelve to about eighteen, the young person has no economic role in an industrial society (Friedenberg, 1966, pp. 45–56). One of the functions of compulsory schooling and the educational system is to keep the adolescent out of the labor market. This, of course, does not mean that there aren't other functions of the educational system, but it does mean that this is a latent function of that institution.

In early industrial societies, scarcity and the demand for unskilled labor required that young people enter the labor market at an early age and also required a pattern of deferred gratification if one was to achieve middle-class goals. However, with automation and abundance, the pattern was reversed. Adolescents had to be kept out of the labor market, and the deferred gratification pattern became weakened. Since it was possible to achieve middle-class goals without going to work early and saving, a new style of life evolved for adolescents based upon later entry into the labor market and gratification now (Cohen, 1967, p. 204).

These changes also began to change the educational system. One of the key methods of control, the threat of expulsion, was no longer available, since it was necessary to keep everyone in school if at all possible. An educational system stressing discipline and authority fitted the young for the needs of a growing economy in the early stages of industrialization. But with automation and increasing affluence, the Protestant Ethic began to change to the Social Ethic, and the schools also began to change. Discipline, authority, and deferred gratification became structurally less meaningful and more difficult to enforce in mature industrial society (Cohen, 1967, p. 205).

These changes placed the adolescent in a strange position. He was denied any meaningful economic function since there were no jobs available for him. In a society based upon jobholding, the adolescent was denied the main method of gaining self-acceptance. Having no economic role in a job-oriented society is not to be taken seriously (Friedenberg, 1966).

Psychologically, the period of adolescence is one characterized by an absence of enduring commitments, a continuing focus on questions of morality and ideology, and a preoccupation with questions of identity. It is a period in which the young person attempts to establish a mode of interaction with the opposite sex and attempts to break the childhood dependence upon parents (Keniston, 1968, pp. 259–260).

Sociologically, adolescence is characterized by a lack of the adult roles so crucial to self-acceptance in this society: a meaningful economic role through jobholding and a meaningful sexual role through marriage. Adolescents are not involved in the institutions of occupation and marriage (Keniston, 1968, pp. 259–260).

Adolescence, then, amounts to a period of limbo with no

meaningful sociological position in the society and a host of confusing psychological problems. The resulting chaos leads to much discussion of the "problems of youth" and "juvenile delinquency." Adolescents become perceived as a problem simply because they are adolescents.

In this situation, there emerged in the 1950s a youth culture, centered around the high schools, which acted as a sort of buffer between adolescents and the outside world. This youth culture, however, was not in opposition to the existing society, but was rather encouraged and accepted by adult society. It revolved around the rather silly "teenager" role which involved a great emphasis on automobiles, driving around, social acceptance, and conformity to the latest clothing fads. In many ways, participation in this youth culture was good training for a future as a consumer living in an American suburb. One could argue that this youth culture was, in fact, controlled and defined by the interests of American business (B. Berger, 1971, pp. 51–53).

Although some of the activities of teenagers resulted in what is often referred to as "middle-class juvenile delinquency" and parents often complained about this, in general the behavior of teenagers was in accordance with the wishes of their parents that they be socially acceptable. The early rock music which emerged during this period was not protest music, but rather stressed the particular concerns and problems of adolescents.

As we move into the postindustrial period, especially in the decade of the sixties, automation and affluence increase, and the period of time in which the young are kept out of the labor market also increases. Sometimes this is referred to as an increased period of adolescence but it may make more sense to look at the years from the age of eighteen to about twenty-six or even thirty as a new period which differs from adult status but also differs from adolescence. Keniston has called this the youth period.

Youth is a new category created by modern, affluent societies. It is characterized by psychological adulthood without any meaningful participation in adult institutions. The youth is psychologically adult but is sociologically similar to an adolescent (Keniston, 1968, pp. 264–272). That is, while he has passed through most of the psychological problems of adolescence, he is still not involved in the adult institutions of occupation and marriage. Since the youth is not involved in the activities of occupation, his social status is still in limbo, and his social situation does not make the job-oriented values of industrial capitalism meaningful to him in an existential way.

During this period, the young have passed through their identity crisis, have begun to establish an ideology, and have dealt with their relationship to the opposite sex. Increasing affluence and automation make it possible for them to stay out of the labor market for a longer period of time, and a new set of educational institutions arises to make this legitimate. College becomes a necessity, graduate schools increase in size, agencies such as the Peace Corps and VISTA arise. The period in which the young do not have a vested interest in existing adult institutions increases. During this time, the youth seeks to develop a basic outlook on the world and a sense of himself. Not having a vested interest in existing institutions and not being required to play adult roles, he is more likely to question existing institutions and his relationship to them. That is, his relation to existing social reality is not grounded in the sort of existential participation that would enable it to appear solid or become objectified.

As with the development of any new style of life, not everyone in the eighteen-to-thirty age group goes through a youth period. Since about half the persons who are eighteen do not go to college, removal from the labor force at this age is not universal. It is primarily the most affluent and most talented persons who are allowed this luxury (Keniston, 1968, pp. 272–273). Only a minority stays out of adult institutions for the entire period. However, those who do go through this period have a long period of time in which they are free of some of the psychological problems of adolescence and are also free of the role requirements of adults. In addition, they are usually in institutions such as universities, which encourage a critical approach to the world. Thus, during this time, the young question social institutions and their relationship to them. Social reality becomes transparent, and institutions reified by others become problematic. This provides the possibility of a collective redefinition of the social world.

Although only a minority of the young go through this prolonged youth period, their numbers are increasing. In addition, those who are questioning and probing institutions are in situations where they are interacting with large masses of young people, and the questioning of the few evolve into the doubts of the many. The number of people kept out of the job market past the age of eighteen has become a significant mass.

In earlier periods of industrialization, the main thrust for social change came from the working population through unions and the like. The working class, however, became absorbed through higher wages and better working conditions and lost much of its critical nature. Further, increasing affluence allowed greater satisfaction of the basic needs, and this in turn increased the potential emphasis on the self needs. However, in order to begin to probe the problems of the self needs, persons must have time free from the necessity of earning a living. Also, in order to see through the web of mystifications that maintain social institutions and to recognize the existence of the universal fake-out, an opportunity to look at these institutions while not having a vested interest in them is necessary. In this sense, students rather than workers are better placed for social criticism. In addition, for the first time in history, the number of persons over the age of eighteen who are not in the labor force has become large enough to make these persons an important interest group within the society.

For instance, in 1939, the number of workers in the coal and railroad industries was 1,376,000, while the number of college students was 1,350,000. In 1968, by contrast, the number of workers in coal and railroads was 715,900, while the number of college students had increased to 7,000,000. During the important decade of the sixties, the number of college students doubled. As White (1969) has pointed out, students now outnumber farmers 3 to 1, miners 50 to 1, and railway workers 9 to 1. To some degree, then, students have become the largest single-interest group in the country. That is, technological change has placed a large number of young people in a situation where they are interacting with others of about the same age and share a common problem in their relation to the economic system.

In addition, as we noted earlier, there is within the student population an increasing number of persons in their middle and late twenties. These are not adolescents but rather persons who are psychologically adult but free of adult social roles. It is this mass of young people, then, that becomes the focus of a social movement that begins to react to the problems that seem to be innate in industrial societies and begins to seek ways to change existing institutional patterns.

The effect of television and other mass media is to link these seven million persons together and make them more aware of their common interests and problems. During the sixties, there began to emerge a conception of students as a special sort of class with special sorts of problems. A group identity slowly emerged; eventually a polemic defining students as niggers appeared and became a manifesto for creating group identity. This is the culmination of a process that has been going on for some time as the changing nature of college education has led to an increased feeling of a group identity among college students.

The growth of the industrial-technological meritocracy and the increasing part played in the meritocracy by college education and, even more, by the college degree, have changed the earlier traditions of colleges and universities in American society and in much of the Western world. College life is no longer simply an extension of family ties and friendship ties. College life is no longer simply a time of adolescent high-jinks, of fun and games. Unlike elementary and high school education, which are still very largely felt by the students to be "unreal" and to be fun and games, college life is now part of the "real world." It is no longer an "identity moratorium." It is a very practical activity for most people and is seen as having great bearing on their whole social identities. . . . college life has come to be seen as increasingly important in the lives of the students, as increasingly the source of status, and not merely as adjunct to status. It is no longer an ivory tower, but a place of very practical work. Rather than a time in life for songs of youthful *Weltschmerz* and moonlight serenades, it is increasingly a place of hard work and of anguish over status, of anguish over whether one will get into graduate school or professional school, or will get the "right" government or corporation job. College has increasingly become a source of shared interest and shared problems *in itself* for students. Rather than being an extension of outside social relations and social status, the college and university has increasingly become a way of transforming outside social relations and social status. The outside world has become more an adjunct to the college and university, at least *as students see it,* whether it is true or not. There is every practical reason for taking one's membership in the college community, one's *identity* as a *"college student,"* as an increasingly important part of one's social position, as the individual himself defines that social position, and, therefore, becomes an increasingly important basis for the development of a subculture—and a class. [Douglas, 1970, pp. 63–64]

The development of group identity among college students, then, reflects the fact that the period of time spent in educational institutions has become an increasingly important part of the lives of these people. Besides their removal from the labor market, students are also characterized by their general affluence.

But this is precisely where the immediate economic class interests of the college students dovetail with and reinforce their broader class interests, their distinctive style-of-life interests. This is not merely a new class, it is, more specifically, a *new leisure class*. College students, especially those from the upper and upper-middle classes, who predominate at the "elite colleges," have been the first *large* group of people in the history of American society—and the world—to be truly affluent. As they themselves so often insist, they are the affluent generation—the post-depression, post-war, welfare generation. They have been free of work and free of most economic worries all their lives. They have spent much of their lives lolling before television sets, dating, going to the beach, and doing whatever seemed like fun at the time: "If it feels good, do it." Fun and freedom have become their gods, their values, their way of life. They have lived in leisure cultures and devoted themselves to entertainment cultures for most of their adolescent lives, though those bound for the "elite schools" have in recent years had to resentfully devote some more time to competing for grades during schooltime. They have not merely been treated permissively by their parents; they have been indulged, freed from almost all household tasks by hard-working mothers who spent considerable time driving them around to their parties when they were children and helping them prepare for dates or parties when they were older. [Douglas, 1970, p. 65]

Modern American society, then, has created a large group of persons raised in affluence, aware of the world through the mass media, turned on by over fifteen years of exposure to rock music (the effects of which have not been clearly determined), intrigued by the ideas of Marx, Freud, Watts, Mills, and other critics of existing institutions, and bombarded by the availability of a number of consciousness-changing chemicals.

A large, affluent population with its basic needs met and with a critical attitude toward social institutions begins to turn toward ways of satisfying self needs. Given a set of institutions that does not allow satisfaction of such needs, a search begins for new patterns of behavior. It is in the gap between the ideology of existing institutions, and the existential situation and activities of a significant mass of young people, that a new social reality begins to emerge. However, the values adopted by the new culture have their roots in the past history of western societies and are a secondary value-system for the parents of these young people.

That is, the new social reality does not emerge from thin air and is not totally the product of an age group but is also a product of a special portion of the middle class that itself is a result of technological change.

The group that becomes the basis for a mass movement aimed at transforming industrial societies is characterized mainly by the age of its members. However, our previous discussion suggests that the social class of its members is also important to this group. How different, then, are the affluent young from their parents? How different are they from their working-class agemates?

Analysis of a recent survey by CBS News sheds some light on these questions. In Table 1, I have selected several questions from this survey that deal with attitudes toward some of the basic values of industrial society. The respondents in this survey were college youth, parents of college youth, noncollege youth, and parents of noncollege youth. This is roughly equivalent to a crosstabulation by age and social class, since most college youth and their parents come from the upper-middle class, and noncollege youth and their parents are more likely to come from the working class.

The data from this survey indicate that parents of noncollege youth are most committed to the statements supporting organized religion, hard work, patriotism, and conventional morality, while college youth are the least committed. The other two groups fall in between the ones just mentioned in their commitment to mainstream values. This is about what we would expect. However, notice that while the college youth group is the most extreme, on some issues they are closer to their noncollege agemates than to either adult group, while on other issues they are closer to their parents than to either of the working class groups. That is, younger people in general tend to be more "liberal" on these issues than older people. At the same time, "liberalism" on questions of tolerance and social issues is directly related to social class so that the more affluent are more liberal on these sorts of questions than the less affluent.

TABLE 1
Values of Industrial Capitalism

	PERCENT AGREE			
	PARENTS OF NON-COLLEGE YOUTH	PARENTS OF COLLEGE YOUTH	NON-COLLEGE YOUTH	COLLEGE YOUTH
Hard work will always pay off.	85	76	79	56
Organized religion is important to me.	91	81	71	42
Patriotism is very important.	—	—	60	35
Abortion is morally wrong.	66	50	64	36
Homosexuality is morally wrong.	79	63	72	42
Premarital sex is morally wrong.	88	74	57	34
There is too much concern with equality and too little concern with law and order (strongly agree).	59	42	48	17

Taken from Daniel Yankelovich, *Generations Apart: A Study of The Generation Gap Conducted for CBS News* (New York: Columbia Broadcasting System, 1969). From *Public Opinion: Changing Attitudes on Contemporary Political and Social Issues,* 1972, R. R. Bowker Company.

That is, college youth appear to come from a family setting that promotes a set of values somewhat different than those considered mainstream in American society. A closer look at the relation between social class and liberalism may be helpful.

Research has indicated that while liberalism, when defined as support of the welfare state, is inversely related to social class, liberalism on civil rights, civil liberties, and internationalism is directly related to social class as measured by income, occupational prestige, and especially education (Kelly and Chambliss, 1966). There is, in general, a greater tolerance for alternative lifestyles and a stronger emphasis on free speech and support of the right to dissent among higher-income groups than among lower-income groups.

A recent public-opinion poll demonstrates this further. Among all whites in the United States, 48 percent are in favor of "helping blacks move faster to achieve equality" while 35 percent are opposed to this. Among people with incomes over $15,000, the statement receives support by a wider 58-to-30 margin. On student dissent, the difference is even more striking. Persons with incomes under $10,000 believe that campus protests are "not a good thing" by a margin of 56-to-26 percent, while persons with incomes over $15,000 see student demonstrations as a "healthy sign" by 53-to-38 percent. A majority of 53 percent of the over-$15,000 group do not see the danger of drugs and pornography as a serious risk associated with going to college, while the under-$10,000 group see this as a real threat by a 60-to-30 margin. The most affluent group is also the most dovish on Vietnam.

All of this suggests that among a subgroup of the upper-middle class there exists a generally tolerant, socially liberal, humanistic value-system. This may be relegated to a secondary status in the lives of the people involved due to pressures to succeed and continue to thrust upward in the economic system, but the value-system is passed on to the children of this group who then, through their removal from the labor force, have an opportunity to attempt to form a lifestyle around these values. College youth, then, reflect the combined influence of their parents and their age group. They are not so much rebelling against their parents' values as intensifying them and extending them while in the critical environment of the university. The "gap" here is not just a generation gap. It is also a gap between the social liberalism of the affluent and the social conservatism of the working class.

The counter-culture of the young began at the most prestigious universities among the most affluent young and eventually spread to the more general college youth population. It does not yet appear to have spread to the noncollege young who do not have the same base of affluence.

In the critical environment of the university, then, affluent youth already oriented to the liberalism of their parents began to form a counter-culture as a reaction to some of the characteristics of industrial society.

It appears that technological change and the production of affluence is creating a portion of the upper middle class with a secondary value-system that stresses social liberalism and humanism. At the same time, technological change removes the children of this group from the labor force for an extended period of time. To see how a youth movement might develop under these conditions, it might be useful to compare this situation with the situation in societies undergoing a transformation from the agricultural stage to the industrial stage, since youth movements generally arise in these societies.

Student movements are expected in societies where traditional authority is disintegrating under the impact of industrialization and modernization and where families adhere to traditional culture (Eisenstadt, 1956). This leads to a disjunction between the values of the family and those in larger society. University students in agrarian societies find themselves in a situation in which ecological changes are undermining the former values and the former traditional authorities. New authority and values have yet to be legitimized. The youth movements arise as a means of providing adaptation to the conditions of industrialization and of developing and accepting the values of rationalism, democracy, and so forth, which they were not provided in their traditional families.

The movement to develop this new value-system finds its

base in the overproduction of educated youth for whom there is the possibility of unemployment because there are insufficient jobs in the areas in which they have trained. Political authority builds a university system for technical progress but resists the cultural changes necessary to enter the industrial age. These cultural values develop in future-oriented youth movements.

Essentially, then, as Flacks (1970) notes, cultural disintegration, an overpopulation of the educated, reactionary regimes, and university conditions lead to the rise of youth movements in societies undergoing the transformation from agrarian to industrial production. In this view, youth movements should not occur in stable industrial societies.

Yet, as we have been emphasizing throughout this book, just such a youth movement has developed in advanced industrial societies. It has all the characteristics of "classical" youth movements, stressing the moral superiority of youth, antiauthoritarianism, equality, and social transformation.

One way to explain the rise of youth movements in advanced industrial societies is to see them as last-gasp reactions to the industrial age that are attempting romantically to recapture the past. This type of explanation has been offered by several analysts, all of whom are somewhat hostile to the youth culture. This explanation does not seem especially convincing, especially since, as I have tried to indicate, the counter-culture is in many ways consistent with the ecological conditions of advanced industrial societies.

Flacks (1970) has suggested that the present youth movements may well represent an attempt to develop a set of values for a new period of history and, rather than being retrogressive, may well signal the type of cultural system which will come to prevail in the postindustrial period.

As I noted earlier, the present student movement originated at the "best" colleges among the "brightest" students and has at its core the liberal, humanistic values of the parents of these students. "The student movement originated among those young people who came out of what might be called the 'intellectual' or 'humanist' subculture of the middle class" (Flacks, 1970). It has spread from there with the development of the youth culture.

Flacks notes that youth from this subculture of the middle class might well experience a discontinuity between the intellectual, humanist values of their families and the reality of competitive industrial capitalism. His studies of the parents of student activists show a strong commitment to intellectuality, unusual political awareness, strong political liberalism, and skepticism about conventional middle-class lifestyles and values. This is similar to the analysis I have presented above.

Students from these families, then, were likely to find educational institutions rigid and authoritarian, and to respond to an analysis such as *The Student As Nigger* (Farber, 1969). Further, they were likely to see the educational system as an extension of the larger institutional system and have difficulties relating to this.

Although expressed in a different way, the affluent young in an advanced industrial society experience a disjunction between family values and societal "reality" simliar to the young in modernizing societies. However, instead of a disjunction between traditional and industrial value systems, the disjunction is between industrial and humanistic value-systems (Flacks, 1970).

Likewise, although there is not an overproduction of educated youth in industrial societies in the same sense as in modernizing ones, the contrived nature of the available jobs and their tendency to turn all activity into labor work leads to a tendency on the part of the humanistic young to resist integration into the occupational structure as long as possible.

There is also recent evidence that, in addition, the educational system has produced too many teachers, engineers, and Ph.D.s for the available positions. Thus, the once-open market for newly minted Ph.D.s has been transformed into a Ph.D. glut, and college graduates at all degree levels are faced with the possibility of being "obsolete."

When combined with the decreased relevance of extrinsic rewards in an affluent society, the humanistic skepticism of their families, the unavailability or irrelevance of jobs leads to a youth group unable to relate to existing institutions in a meaningful way. The youth culture arises to fill the resulting gap. Any condition which leads to a weakening of motivation for upward mobility increases the likelihood of student rebellion.

From the intellectuals, with the development of the humanities and social sciences, a critique of industrial capitalism has been developing for some time. The last generation attempted to humanize the society and provide equal opportunity through the welfare state. Their offspring, who reached the nation's campuses during the 1960s in large numbers, at first tried to work pretty much the same way. However, the failure of the civil rights movement to bring equality for blacks, the war in Vietnam, and the discovery that affluence did not usher in an age of happiness, led to a youth movement that began to question the underlying assumptions of industrial capitalism.

This, in many ways, is consistent with the prediction conservative economist Schumpeter (1950) made nearly thirty years ago. Schumpeter felt that the affluence produced by capitalism would lead to an expanded educational system and an increasing number of intellectuals, who in their usual complaining way would attack the cultural manifestations of capitalism and lead to its demise. This is essentially what appears to be happening, except that the criticism is not just aimed at capitalism but at the entire way of life of advanced industrial societies, regardless of their specific form: the Soviet system is subject to the same attack leveled against the American system.

It should be clear that most of the analysis of this book leads to the same conclusions as those of Schumpeter and Flacks. Basic changes in values are required to cope with an abundant society, and the present youth movements represent an attempt to develop and define such a value-system, based upon the humanistic values that have been around in western societies for some time but have never had a chance to flower in practice since ecological conditions were not consistent with their practice.

If an alternative or counter-culture is emerging among the affluent young, we would naturally want to know what are the characteristics of that culture and how it differs from the culture of mainstream industrial capitalism. I will now compare the two cultures and try to show how each derives from the activities of the groups that create and maintain them.

SIX

The Alternative Culture:
The Social Reality of
the Leisure Class

In the last chapter, we saw that a large number of young people are allowed a legitimate release from the labor market for an increasing period of their lives. The social reality created by that group of persons in the course of their day-to-day activities would be expected, over the course of time, to become rather different from that of those mainly engaged in activities performed within the labor market. I will now try to analyze the differences between mainstream culture and the alternative life style, or counter-culture, emerging among youth groups.

Youth Culture as a Response to
Postindustrial Society

Contemporary youth culture may be viewed as a response to the incongruity of the values of work (occupation) and scarcity with an emergent social organization characterized by abundance or the lack of scarcity.

The nature of this response and its connection to changing

ecological conditions can be seen by a comparison of the dominant themes of what we will call "mainstream industrial culture" with the dominant themes of the youth culture or counter-culture.

It is, of course, difficult to describe the context of something as amorphous as a youth movement. This is especially so since the "movement" actually consists of several movements. Further, any particular aspect of the youth culture may not be accepted by all youth who consider themselves part of that culture. Despite these difficulties, *it is possible to identify some aspects of the youth culture that differentiate it from the mainstream industrial culture*. Various writers have identified some of the characteristics of the youth culture. One way to combine these aspects into an overall analysis is to *look at certain key features of industrial culture and note how the youth culture differs from these*. Of course, dividing these up in this manner is arbitrary and there is, in reality, a great deal of overlap between values. In fact, we will see that one group of values tends to cluster together to form the industrial culture while another group clusters to form the youth culture. This tendency for a group of values to cluster together is due to the human need for cognitive consistency. The result is an overall *Weltanschauung* through which a person sees and interprets events around him. Because of this, if the overall worldviews of two persons differ significantly, they will have difficulty communicating. We will look at six key cultural aspects in order to identify the crucial characteristics of the youth culture.

SCARCITY

The structure of industrial society is based upon the assumption of scarcity. Industrial economics is the science that deals with the distribution of scarce resources. The structure is competitive, based on a zero-sum game which assumes that if one player gains, another necessarily loses. This is most evident in regard to economic matters but also intrudes into other areas.

For instance, if a man "loves" one woman, he cannot "love" another without losing some of his "love" for the first. One only has so much "love" to distribute. This zero-sum model pits men against each other in competition for scarce resources, whether they be economic, emotional, or psychological (Slater, 1970, pp. 96–118).

The youth culture, on the other hand, is geared to abundance because it takes abundance for granted. Reared in an affluent environment, middle-class youth assume that their basic needs will be met. General affluence and the presence of credit buying have undermined the deferred-gratification pattern of the past. It is no longer necessary to put off pleasure now in order to be successful in the future (competition between use of resources now or later). Consequently, wants can be, or should be, satisfied now.

The demands of minority groups for a decent standard of living are not seen as threatening the economic well-being of middle-class youth, since it is assumed that the society could easily provide a decent standard of living for everyone.

Abundance is taken for granted in other areas, such as the emotional and psychological. Love is not something to be hoarded or rationed but, rather, something to be distributed as widely as possible since loving one person does not prevent one from loving someone else.

The assumption of scarcity or the assumption of abundance affects a person's entire way of life and his way of looking at the world. It is a central aspect of the difference between the mainstream culture and the youth culture. It is not just that middle-class youth have lived with abundance while their parents had to deal with scarcity. The youth culture has developed a value-system which does not see economic wants as unlimited and, therefore, can interpret abundance as a level of living that mainstream culture would not characterize as such.

This can best be understood if we recognize the difference between a naturalistic interpretation of scarcity and a sociocultural interpretation. Scarcity can be defined as "any limitation of 'resources' assertedly necessary to actualize any given valued end in the form of behavior relevant to concrete social situations" (Stanley, 1968, p. 856). A sociocultural perspective toward scarcity recognizes that a perception of scarcity in a culture contains two elements: a physical or natural condition, and a social definition of that condition as involving or not involving scarcity. That is, there is an objective condition and a subjective interpretation of that condition.

If one assumes a "natural" condition of scarcity, as most economists do, then one is bound by an assumption of iron determinism. However, if one recognizes the subjective element of scarcity, then he can gain a relative freedom of choice that he would otherwise not have (Stanley, 1968, p. 856).

The youth culture invokes a different subjective definition of a given level of living than does the mainstream culture. Rather than seeing the lack of a high standard of living as scarcity, the alternative culture sees a scarcity of opportunity for the free exercise of human activities in the assumption that economic goods are scarce far beyond the level of a reasonably comfortable standard of living.

Once a subjective definition that asserts the existence of abundance in both the economic and psychological realms exists in a culture, the people who live in that culture have a greater ability to engage in cooperative activity and to ignore the competitive model of interaction. If there exist sufficient economic goods to meet the basic needs of everyone, and if self-acceptance is not a limited commodity but rather is possible for everyone, then the zero-sum competitive model makes little or no sense.

It can be seen from the above that in the assumption of scarcity or abundance, there is an enormous gap between the subjective definition of the alternative culture and that of mainstream culture. This results in a large difference in *Weltanschauung* between the two cultures and a corresponding difference in approach to practically every human activity.

WORK

The value of work (labor work rather than leisure work) is central to industrial societies: "a hard day's work well done" is glorified in song and cliché. No one should have the right to consume if he does not produce. A man's identity is determined by his occupation, and his social status is allocated accordingly. While the work ethic is weakening somewhat in mainstream society, it is still stressed heavily. Thus, an American President promotes a welfare revision which would double the number of welfare recipients as "workfare." He who will not work is a bum, to be distinguished from those who are needy because they are unable to find jobs or are unable to work. The emphasis on the value of work exists among all elements of mainstream culture regardless of whether they call themselves conservatives or liberals.

The work ethic is, of course, closely linked to the assumption of scarcity. If consumer goods are scarce, it is, of course, necessary that everyone work in order to ensure that enough is produced. If enough can be produced to satisfy basic needs without everyone working, then it doesn't make sense to insist that everyone do so. In the affluence-based youth culture, work becomes much less important. Youth are kept out of the labor market as long as possible and have never developed the "need to work" through existential experience, which comes about through forming work habits. Consequently, whether one works or not isn't very important. "It's not what you do that's important, it's what you are." Thus, the admonition to "get a job" does not impress those whose allegiance is to the youth culture. This, of course, creates a great deal of antagonism toward the alternative culture since, in the worldview of mainstream culture, there is no provision for this sort of attitude.

GUILT

Industrial society insists that a person live up to the image of a decent person emphasized in its social reality. "Acceptable persons do not have unacceptable desires" (Putney and Putney, 1964, p. 7). "Unacceptable" desires are to be denied and a person should feel guilty for having them. A good sense of guilt is seen as necessary for social order and productivity. The public self that one learns to project is evaluated by how closely it fits the societal ideal image. Indirect self-acceptance is sought, and the search for this becomes the driving force in a person's life.

The youth culture rejects the notion of feeling guilty about unacceptable desires and accepts instead the idea that "nothing human is alien to me." The emphasis is more on obtaining direct self-acceptance through full disclosure of the self than on obtaining indirect self-acceptance through matching the ideal societal image. The value-system of the alternative culture justifies and legitimizes this mode of gaining self-acceptance. It would not be possible for persons to gain self-acceptance this way if there were not contained within the social reality of the alternative culture the notion that this is the proper way to obtain self-acceptance. Guilt and shame are seen not as essential to maintaining social order, but rather as harmful hangups that should be done away with. This does not mean that youth are always successful in eliminating guilt, only that this is the goal and that this goal is different from the one emphasized in mainstream society.

AUTHORITY

The acceptance of rational-legal authority is essential to the organization of industrial society. "Respect for authority" is venerated in political speeches, newspaper editorials, television shows, and the *National Review*. Authority figures are those persons who have been certified as expert or knowledgeable in some area through experience and training. It is not a person's charismatic nature that gives him authority, but rather the position he occupies. Thus, one must "respect the President" or other high governmental authority, and in our decent town "the kids here still respect the college dean."

Acceptance of rational-legal authority, however, entails a cost, since we must often then do something we do not want to do. This is offset by rewards controlled and allocated by persons in positions of authority. Since most rewards in industrial society are tied to the economic system, such rewards are only effective if they are scarce. As satisfying basic needs becomes fairly easy and taken for granted, rewards based upon such needs become less meaningful. Rewards based on indirect satisfaction of the self needs become less relevant as persons seek direct self-acceptance. Thus, persons in positions of authority find it increasingly difficult to evoke respect from youth. The rewards they offer in return for such respect are decreasing in value. Not understanding this, since the rewards they offer have a great deal of value to themselves, persons in positions of authority react with anger when they do not receive the respect they feel is due them.

The youth culture places less emphasis on the rational-legal basis of a person's authority derived from the position he occupies and emphasizes more the equal status of all persons in a decision-making process.

RATIONALITY

The rational bureaucratic form of organization characteristic of industrial societies requires that all phenomena be viewed "objectively" in accordance with a set of given rules. Thus, persons are dealt with in a bureaucratic organization not on personalistic grounds but through the application of universalistic standards. This form of organization is legitimized by the scientific worldview. This worldview requires that all phenomena—be they persons, events, the environment, or whatever—be divided into objects that can be typed and classified and thus dealt with in a scientific, objective manner.

This way of viewing the world is efficient in terms of production and progress. It is, of course, responsible for much of the technological progress and scientific advance of industrial societies. However, it does mean that a person's relationships with other persons and with the environment are fragmented into a relationship between "in-here" and "out-there," an alienating relationship in which "objects" are to be manipulated and conquered (Roszak, 1969, pp. 205–238).

The youth culture replaces the rational-scientific worldview with one based on personalistic relationships with other persons and a holistic relation with the environment. Thus, a person is seen as part of a *Gestalt* that includes other persons and the environment, instead of a separate "ego" located in a bag of skin. This worldview is legitimated by mysticism and magic. This worldview is certainly less efficient than the scientific one, but it reduces the alienating features of industrial society.

COMMITMENT

Most persons in any society do not question the underlying assumptions of that society—in fact, they are not even aware of these assumptions. The social reality in which they live, thus, provides meaning for their lives and goals to seek. Due to the pluralism of industrial societies, the underlying assumptions of these societies are more apparent than in preindustrial societies (Kelly, 1972). Still, as I noted earlier, existing institutions are taken seriously, and there is great commitment to the goals of the society. Social reality is viewed as reasonably firm and solid. The flag is more than a piece of cloth: it is something to be displayed proudly and to which to be committed.

The youth culture, on the other hand, takes an ironic, irreverent view of institutions and constantly questions the assumptions of the society. Social reality is more transparent, and much of life is seen as a game. If institutions change, this is not a great threat since they weren't taken seriously anyway. This attitude invokes a great deal of hostility toward the young, since nothing angers a man more than having someone laugh at that which provides meaning to his life.

This does not mean that the counter-culture is free from reification. Some of its own social reality becomes reified, especially in the political wing of the movement. This, of course, will always happen, since any alternative social reality is created the same way as the mainstream reality. However, in general, there is more skepticism and less commitment in the youth culture than in mainstream culture.

In general, then, mainstream industrial society is organized in a rational, bureaucratic manner in order to perform labor work which is deemed necessary to deal with scarcity. Its driving force is indirect self-acceptance which is sought through upward mobility in a competitive lifestyle. The counter-culture, based on abundance and freed from task orientation, is more loosely organized and personalistic. Mainstream culture is geared to economic production through activities organized as jobs performed for extrinsic rewards. The counter-culture is geared to satisfaction of human needs (especially self needs) and stresses activities performed for intrinsic reasons. Free of scarcity assumptions and the consequent need for productive efficiency, the counter-culture can stress a more expressive, cooperative lifestyle than does mainstream culture. One cannot say that one or the other of these lifestyles is superior, since that is a value-judgment and depends on what the lifestyle is intended to achieve. It does, however, appear that the counter-culture is more in tune with the ecological realities of postindustrial society and might therefore suggest the form into which postindustrial society will evolve.

Conclusions

I have tried to show that present youth movements reflect a stage of ecological development that allows emphasis on activities performed for their own sake and justified by a humanistic ideological system. For any group to engage primarily in intrinsically rewarding activities and to stress a humanistic value-system as its *primary* value-system, that group must enjoy affluence and a legitimate release from the labor market. Affluence and release from the labor market permit persons to engage in activities for their own sake and to develop a value-system which derives from, is consistent with, and provides justification for, those activities. It is through the activities that men perform that the existential link between ecological conditions and values can be found.

This is not to suggest that the value-system found in the counter-culture is new. Most of these values have been around for some time and represent a *secondary* value-system for the parents of many persons in the youth culture (Slater, 1970, pp. 96–118). Further, similar value-orientations have appeared in past youth movements.

The hippies, and their immediate antecedents, the Beats, were in good part direct descendants of the ancient Bohemian subcultures of various kinds that have existed in Western cultures for centuries and can already be found referred to in Benvenuto Cellini's *Autobiography*. It would no doubt be possible to trace the direct lines of descent in terms of ideas and persons from the romantic Bohemian subcultures of early nineteenth-century France up to such present day groups as the hippies. While various schools of artists, who are very often intermingled with members of the Bohemian subcultures, have adopted both favorable and unfavorable orientations toward involvement in the work ethic and the rationalistic, bourgeois society, the *Bohemian cultures, including the hippie culture today, are characterized by a basic rejection of this work-a-day world and an idealization of the opposite values of leisure, feeling, idealism, and so on.* Their attacks on formal education, industrial society, Christian purity, and the rationalistic discipline of scientific thought have been unrelenting; and, while we certainly have no reliable quantitative information on such things, there is no reason to believe that the (hard core) members of these leisure subcultures today are larger in proportion to the general population (indeed, they may be smaller today) or attract more general sympathy and public interest today than they did in the nineteenth century. Just as many hard-working, straight bourgeoisie today adopt hippie beads or smoking habits, so did bankers' wives read the romantic novels in the nineteenth century; and there were undoubtedly week-end Bohemians comparable to our weekend hippies. It is probably precisely because these leisure cultures have been so different from our everyday lives that they have always generated so much interest. As members of our society generally see such things, they are generally an "escape," not a program for the future. [Douglas, 1970, pp. 48–49]

Given the characteristics of the workaday world that I discussed earlier, it is not surprising that there are recurring movements that tend to reject that world. There is a tendency among some investigators to dismiss a social movement if it appears to be repeating the behavior of past movements. Instead, we should recognize that repeated attempts to escape from the workaday world may suggest that there is something wrong with that world. We need also to be aware that, despite the obvious similarities, social movements that take place at different times are not exactly the same. At the same time, we need to avoid the tendency to see the present behavior of youth as a new wave that necessarily represents the future. Some of the phenomena now taking place have happened before.

In addition, historically, youth movements have appeared and prospered only against a background of rising affluence and characteristically are middle-class phenomena. What I am emphasizing here is that the technology of postindustrial societies allows the development and expression of humanistic values among a large number of young people, and that the conditions that make this possible are likely to spread both to a greater number of persons under twenty-five and to persons in an increasing age-range as automation allows persons to stay out of the labor market for longer periods of time. Only as both the subculture definition of the existence of abundance and consequent decreased need to hold a job become general characteristics in the larger population, would we expect the value-system of the counter-culture to become primary and the value-system associated with industrial capitalism to become secondary.

It is important to remember that some of the behavior associated with the counter-culture derives from the fact that, at present, this value-complex is tied to a youth movement. Youth movements have always been extreme, emotional, enthusiastic; they have never been moderate or rational. They have always held a conviction that the established order was corrupt to the core and beyond redemption. They have always predicted doom for the existing order and have regarded the present generation as the first and last in history. Much of the reaction to the present youth movements derives from these characteristics. Often overlooked is the fact that the value-system that exists in the counter-culture is a product of the past history of western societies, and that the ecological conditions that allow expression of that value-system as a primary one are also a product of those same societies.

It is not the youth movements themselves or the characteristics that are always associated with youth movements that are more important here, but rather the fact that the humanistic value-system that has always been present as an ideal may now be congruent with the technological state of postindustrial society, and therefore capable of practice.

SEVEN

The Damning of the Greening: Legitimation of the Alternative Culture

Any social movement, especially if it is aimed at transforming an existing society, will elicit numerous attempts to "explain" the movement and to predict where it is going. This has always been true but is especially so in modern societies in which large numbers of people specialize in social science or mass media attempts to make sense of whatever is going on. The interesting thing about these attempts to explain a movement is that the explanations themselves have a tendency to become part of the movement and often elicit as much response from other interpreters as the movements which they seek to explain.

In 1970 there appeared in the United States a book titled *The Greening of America,* by Charles Reich. A portion of the book appeared in *The New Yorker* and received a great deal of attention. When the book itself appeared, it was reviewed and received a great deal of response in *The New York Times*. It immediately became a bestseller. Book reviews appeared in most of the leading periodicals, and a rather large percentage of these reviews were very critical of the book. The book was accused of advocating the end of reason and postulating the kind of thinking which led to the rise of the Nazis in Germany. (A favorite scare-tactic used by people of all political persuasions is to compare whatever you are attacking to Hitler, the all-purpose symbol of evil.) A *Newsweek* columnist called Reich's book "a scary bag of mush." Whatever else Reich's book accomplished, it became part of the great debate about youth movements and where they were going in modern America. Further, the book seemed to touch some sort of nerve in the population at large, especially in book reviewers for liberal magazines. To attempt to understand why there was such a reaction to *Greening,* both favorable and unfavorable, it might be helpful to look at what Reich said in the book and also at the general characteristics of attempts to explain the youth movement.

The heart of Reich's thesis, and the part of the book that has caused most of the controversy, is his description of three states of consciousness that he feels have characterized the development of the United States. Consciousness I is the world view of small-town America, which stresses the independent individual, small government, and laissez-faire economics. It is the state of consciousness that goes with the family farm, small business, and small-scale manufacturing. According to Reich, this state of consciousness characterized America up to the Depression and the New Deal. Large-scale manufacturing, the rise of corporations, and the corresponding increase in the size of government, brought about the welfare state and Consciousness II. Consciousness II is the liberal, rational worldview that goes with large bureaucracies and the rule of law. This worldview stresses the need for government planning, economic growth, the responsibility of society for all its citizens, etc. It is essentially the worldview of the liberal supporter of the welfare state. Reich emphasizes the negative aspects of this state of consciousness, especially the application of the cult of efficiency to all affairs of life, which leads to destruction of the environment, consumerism, and the burning of villages in Vietnam.

As a response to the inability of Consciousness II to bring

about a human society, Consciousness III arises among the youth of the middle class and it stresses contemplation, creativity, self-actualization, etc. Essentially, we could say that Reich is postulating three myths which were the guiding worldviews at various times: the myth of individual autonomy, the myth of social engineering, and the myth of ecstatic community (Capouya, 1971, pp. 85–86). That is, each of these myths represents the straw-man image of its adherents, and the society which goes with each state of consciousness doesn't necessarily fit exactly the characteristics of the myths. Many critics of Reich have spent most of their time complaining that early America was not really the way it is described in Consciousness I. Of course it wasn't. The point is that a group that subscribes to any of these myths pretends that things are the way the myth says they are and strives to fit the image of the myth. Groups that have different myths will be aiming toward different goals, and will have different visions of proper behavior and different images of how a society "should" run.

There is much about Reich's analysis that could be criticized. For instance, he feels that Consciousness III will sweep the country so that even businessmen, FBI agents, and the like, will come to subscribe to it, and a cultural revolution will more or less automatically take place. This is unlikely, to say the least. There are also many insightful ideas in the book if it is accepted on its own terms and not criticized because it doesn't meet the specifications of a sociological analysis. However, I am not particularly interested in the merits or demerits of the book here. Rather, I am interested in exploring the role of the book in the counter-culture and the adverse reactions to the book.

It seems to me that most of the adverse reactions to the book, and especially the rather shrill screams of some, are a result of the fact that Reich's book tends to legitimize the activities of those associated with the youth culture. That is, Reich provides a set of justifications for the behavior of the young that run counter to the justifications given for most of the behavior of mainstream society. Reich is attacking the legitimating ideology of the liberal welfare state. Essentially, Reich and his critics are engaged in an ideological battle in which they are providing legitimations for different life styles. Reich is not merely analyzing the youth culture; he is clearly advocating the lifestyle of the young as a way of life for the entire society. Further, his descriptions of the different states of consciousness tend to make Consciousness III look like the essence of all that is good and right, while Consciousness II comes off appearing rigid, devoid of life, and even somewhat evil. He does not describe any of the unfavorable aspects of Consciousness III: he does not deal with deviation from the myth of ecstatic community in the same way that he shows how the real world varies from the myth of social engineering. Since most of the people who review books for liberal periodicals would fall in Reich's category of Consciousness II, it is no wonder that they lash back at him, for he is attacking the very meaning of their lives. Their attacks tend to dwell upon the unfavorable aspects of the lifestyle of the young.

This is important in understanding the relation of attempts to explain social movements to the movements themselves. The way of looking at the world that Reich calls Consciousness II is the prevailing worldview of those academics and journalists who write most of the analyses of the youth culture. That is, events which fall outside the accepted behavior of a social reality will be explained in terms of that reality and, thus, neutralized in their impact on that reality. What Reich has done is to turn things around and explain the behavior of mainstream society in the terms of the social reality of the counter-culture. By doing so, he reinforces the reality of the counter-culture and delegitimizes the activities of mainstream society. His critics, in turn, attempt to delegitimize the counter-culture and reaffirm their social reality. The process of legitimation is, of course, very important in the development of a social reality and be-

The Damning of the Greening

comes increasingly so as the reality is passed on to new cohorts of human beings (Berger and Luckmann, 1966, pp. 92–128).

In general, then, there is a tendency for those who are themselves favorable to youth movements to see these movements as saving or revitalizing the world and to stress the moral purity of the young.

Today there are many social prophets who insist with complete certainty that *the* youth movement is this, that, or the other. In many cases these prophecies are very clearly made by radicals and radical sympathizers who are would-be leaders of a Second Great Children's Crusade (though they presumably expect the Crusade to be more successful this time than the first time). They are generally trying to make themselves and others believe that at last the Mighty Host has arrived in the land to set men free from the iniquities of the materialistic life of hard work, competition, and repression. They use wild generalizations about the unity of "the youth movement" and its "totally revolutionary nature" to create an image of strength that will flag floundering spirits, urge the unconvinced to join up before the bandwagon leaves them in the dust (or the "dustbin of history"), and scare their ancient foes into submission: as the bumper sticker says, "America: *Change* It Or *Lose* It." These prophets have hailed the new *Swarmings* of rebellious youth, such as the vast swarming host that turned on and tuned in to the Woodstock Rock Festival, as a third coming, the rise of the New Christianity (only better than last time) that will sweep irresistibly across the land and down through the ages; and, in fact, the radical youth and their adult supporters and users do very frequently make precisely this parallel between the suppressed state of early Christians and the "suppressed" state of youth today (with Chicago as the modern Coliseum), a parallel which even so balanced an analyst as Daniel Moynihan has seen as worthy of consideration in his essay on "Nirvana Now." [Douglas, 1970, p. 59]

The young are portrayed as the last great hope to save a decaying society. Their vision is clear since they haven't yet been corrupted by the corrupt society in which they live. The moral purity of the youth movement will lead to its ultimate triumph over materialistic society.

If a social movement is to be successful in recruiting additional adherents and in changing a society, it must appear to be inevitable and irresistible. Its legitimizers must make it appear to be the wave of the future, which cannot be stopped. We see this clearly in the section of Reich's book that has been conspicuously placed on its jacket.

There is a revolution coming. It will not be like revolutions of the past. It will originate with the individual and with culture, and it will change the political structure only as its final act. It will not require violence to succeed, and it cannot be successfully resisted by violence. This is the revolution of the new generation.

The implication is clear. If the counter-culture's triumph is inevitable, then we had better all jump on the bandwagon or risk being left behind.

The opponents of the counter-culture will tend to delegitimize it in the same way the proponents try to legitimize it. While the proponents will try to make the triumph of the counter-culture appear inevitable, the opponents will stress that the movement is like past youth movements, that it will have no real affect on the existing society, that its adherents are suffering from psychological disturbances, that middle-class youth are merely expressing their boredom in their rather silly behavior, etc. This makes the movement appear to be a rather quaint affair perpetuated by spoiled middle-class youth and their youth-worshipping mentors, a movement in which no thinking person would get involved. The role of legitimations in the struggle between competing social realities is very important.

Thus, we see the youth movement portrayed in a favorable light as the wave of the future by Reich (1970), Roszak (1969), and Slater (1970). We see the same movement portrayed in an unfavorable light that emphasizes what is wrong with the people who are involved in the movement and either dismisses the movement as a fad or sees it as a danger, in the works of Feuer (1969), Lipset (1971), and Nisbet, Starr, and Bromwich (1970). All the writers make some claim about being objective in their analysis, but of course none are. The opponents of the movement especially tend to stress the objective, scientific nature of their analysis (since this is part of their social reality, after all) and to scream with rage if anyone suggests that they are taking an ideological position.

This phenomenon will occur any time we are trying to analyze a movement that is taking place within the social reality in which we live. The persons doing the analysis will be affected by their own tendency to favor the reality of the movement or the reality of the existing society. Thus, the attempts to explain social movements become part of the process of change or attempted change that is going on in the society as they provide legitimations for one or the other social reality. It is very difficult, perhaps even impossible, for an investigator to keep his analysis from becoming part of the legitimizing machinery.

When a social movement is a youth movement, the way people interpret it is also affected by the general stereotypes of youth that exist in the society. Both proponents and opponents will be affected by the tendency either to see young people as embodying all that is pure and good or to see them as barbarians. This is multiplied by the tendency, especially in American society, to stress the sexuality of the young and to be fascinated by it. Novelist Thomas Berger has captured this well in his description of middle-aged Carlo Reinhart with his trusty binoculars watching his neighbor's teenage daughter undress.

He now discerned that nothing was expected of him, he was still in safe hiding, the girl indeed smiled towards him but not at him, seeing nothing but the usual solipsist image of her own youth, vigor, and beauty, mirrored in the blankness of everybody else. She pitched her pants offstage, a movement which caused her firm parts to tremble hardly at all. Reinhart's own trunk had been more tremulous when he tossed his socks aside. In all primary and secondary respects she was full grown, yet not a centimeter, a milligram beyond. She robustly straddled the apex of ripeness. By comparison even the early twenties were already the road to rot. . . . self consciousness would corrupt this glorious and unreflective bestiality. A young girl who thought she knew something was unbearable. [Berger, 1970, pp. 30–31]

The tendency to see the young as sexual animals has been noted by Friedenberg (1966, pp. 50–51). The young are often pictured ambivalently as the possessors of free and unashamed sexuality, and as bestial beings who must be controlled lest their sexuality run rampant. The image is similar to that applied to blacks. Indeed, sexual images of this sort seem to be projected onto out-groups in many societies (Young, 1966).

When the fascination with the young—and especially with the sexuality of the young—that exists in American society is combined with the heavy emphasis on youth in this society and with the ideological factors in the present youth movement, it is no wonder that there has been a great deal written about this movement and that a great deal of heat has been generated. It is also not surprising that a book like *Greening* elicited such an extreme and emotional response.

I have suggested that the explanations of a social movement will themselves be affected by the worldview to which the person giving the explanation subscribes. Further, I have suggested that the attempted explanation tends to either legitimize or de-legitimize the movement. This is true even if the analysis is done by a social scientist who subscribes to the ideal of scientific objectivity. Before he even begins his analysis, he will have chosen a theoretical perspective, and this will greatly affect the results of his analysis.

The theoretical perspectives adopted to explain the movements show all too clearly the ways in which professional disciplines determine one's views of such concrete events and the ways in which theoretical perspectives are adopted long before one comes to such concrete events, so that the theorists have already assumed that they know the general nature of the phenomena and their causes before they come to the concrete phenomena. In the great majority of these works there is an academic presumption that the analyst knows the general truth before he begins. Indeed, in all too many instances there is not merely the assumption that one knows the general nature of the truth, which is certainly more defensible in terms of the impossibility and undesirability of always starting from ground level in trying to understand the world, but there is also the assumption that a great deal is known about the specific nature of the phenomena to be studied. For example, when a structural sociologist comes to study the events of student protest he is very apt to assume completely implicitly that the only valid explanation of the events will be found in the family backgrounds, class associations, or in some other traditionally recognized "structural" factors. In the same way, when a psychologist comes to study the events he is very apt to assume completely implicitly that the only valid explanation of the events will be found in the earlier, especially childhood sexual, family relations of the protesters. The only thing that saves us from a complete war of theoretical perspectives is the willingness of many of the theorists to adopt a multi-factored approach by which they recognize the partial, if subordinate, validity of other perspectives. In this way we get a live-and-let-live approach to the theoretical explanations of the phenomena, but we do not get any closer to the phenomena. The events are forced into the Procrustean bed of preestablished theories and all too often neither the theory nor the events leads to any improvement in the other. [Douglas, 1970, pp. 109–110]

Thus, the training and background of the investigator will predetermine, to a certain extent, which factors he will find important in his analysis of a social movement. Further, as I noted at the beginning of this book, whether or not an investigator assumes that there are basic human needs, whether he starts with an assumption that the present social order is satisfactory, and similar predispositions, will affect the type of analysis that he does and the conclusions he reaches.

When we consider all of the factors which I have discussed in this chapter, it is clear that any analysis of a contemporary social movement will be greatly affected by factors other than the actual characteristics of the movement. Further, since even under the best intentions of objectivity an analysis of a movement tends either to legitimize or to delegitimize it, the social scientist or journalist should be well aware that he is, in some way, becoming part of the process he is describing.

Because of this, the social scientist who is trying to do the best and most objective analysis possible, needs to be aware of the assumptions he is making when he begins his study. These should be stated as clearly as possible so that a reader can then judge the extent to which these assumptions affected the conclusions reached. This is rarely done. It is especially unlikely if an investigator is putting down a social movement through a rather snobbish guise of scientific objectivity. Studies which hide behind the façade of objectivity are probably the least objective of all, since the investigator is not even aware of the factors which are likely to be biasing his study.

It should be fairly obvious that since the present book starts with the assumption that there are basic human needs that are not satisfied under conditions of industrial capitalism, this study tends to legitimize more than delegitimize present youth movements. It does this despite the fact that I have tried to avoid the direct advocacy of a Reich or Roszak. As Becker (1966) has noted, once we are aware of the biases under which we operate and once we have made it clear whose side we are on, we can then do a reasonably objective analysis within those limits. It would greatly improve our knowledge of modern youth movements if all investigators of this subject were to be clear about this. If a trend in this direction begins and gathers strength, some day even Nisbet may admit that he is biased.

EIGHT

The Transition of America: Youth Movements and Social Change

I have suggested that an analysis of a contemporary social movement will always contain some ideological bias since the movement being studied is attempting to bring about a change in the social reality in which we exist. This makes it especially difficult to determine the probability that a social movement will actually bring about the change that it is attempting. One can easily be tempted to see a transition as likely if he desires such a transition, and likewise to see a transition as unlikely if he does not desire a transition or share the goals of the social movement.

When the social movement being studied is a youth movement, the likelihood that it will bring about change is especially difficult to assess. The young have a tendency, which is reinforced to some extent by modern societies, to see their beliefs and lifestyles as the wave of the future. After all, the old will eventually die off, which leaves open the possibility of change as a generational transition takes place. Youth movements seem always to carry the theme that the present society is seriously corrupt largely due to the efforts of the older generation and that things will be purified when the new generation reaches positions of power within the society.

In contrast to this view of change coming about through generational succession, is the view that youth movements as such are not very successful in bringing about change since they lack an independent economic base. In this chapter, I will try to evaluate the likelihood of significant change occurring in modern societies as a result of the present youth movements.

Flacks (1970) has suggested that the emergence of youth movements in advanced industrial societies is a "precursor of major qualitative societal and cultural change." He argues that the youth who are involved in the counter-culture come from a growing subsection of the middle class "composed of persons who have achieved affluence and secure status in occupations oriented to intellectual and cultural work." From his own research and from the analysis of Schumpeter, Flacks concludes that:

The expansion of higher education in our society has produced a social stratum which tends to rear its children with values and character structures which are at some variance with the dominant culture. Affluence and secure status further weaken the potency of conventional incentives and undermine motivations for upward mobility. The outcome of these processes is a new social type or subculture among American youth—humanist youth. [1970, p. 354]

Noting that classical youth movements were indications that traditional, agrarian society was being transformed by processes of industrialization and modernization, Flacks then argues that the appearance of youth movements in advanced industrial societies is a sign that a new cultural and social era is emerging.

. . . the student movement and the new alienated youth culture appear to reflect the erosion, if not the collapse, of what might be called the culture of capitalism—the cluster of values which Max Weber labelled the "Protestant Ethic"—a value system which was appropriate for the development of capitalism and the entrepreneurial spirit which has lost its vitality under the impact of the bureaucratic organization of the economy, the decline of entrepreneurships, and the spread of affluence. The erosion of this culture is reflected in the transformation of family structure and childrearing practices, in the changing relations between the sexes, in the replacement of thrift with consumership as a virtue. As Schumpeter predicted many years ago, bourgeois culture could not survive the abundance it would generate. [1970, p. 355]

Clearly, the erosion of the culture of capitalism would involve a profound change in modern societies, and the suggestion that youth movements reflect such an erosion implies that modern societies are undergoing a transition to a new social reality involving different values and forms of organization.

What are the probabilities that current youth movements will lead to meaningful social change? Are these movements a sign of the transition from industrial to postindustrial society, or are they merely another passing generational phenomena? These questions are difficult to answer. Certainly, there are a number of problems that youth movements have as movements for social change.

Youth movements are transitory. They have no independent socioeconomic base, and the proponents of the movement do not constitute a class, defined in socioeconomic terms. A generational movement usually does not lead to the formation of an actual social group: thus it can lack a structure through which its beliefs and aims could persist over time and consequently have some effect on society. Unlike movements based on social class, generational movements do not provide a reliable and enduring social base for change (Bottomore, 1969, pp. 104–105). Membership in a youth group is temporary; eventually, the former youth leader finds that he is becoming part of the older generation. He who shouts "Don't trust anyone over thirty" soon is himself over thirty.

Colleges, where many youth movements get started, have a very rapid turnover of members. Aside from those who go on to graduate school and the extended "youth" period, colleges lose a substantial number of their students each year; these persons must enter adult occupational roles. Once they leave the university area they scatter, going to different social classes, occupations, and parts of the country; there is no longer any critical group with which all of them can identify. A college is a community of students who live together in the same situation and hold many of the same beliefs, which are continually reinforced through interaction. Upon leaving the university, young people will have difficulty finding reference groups that will allow them to maintain their counter-culture orientation.

Further, adult society expects young people to shape up as they grow older. One social mechanism for neutralizing the effect of radical ideas is to define them as proper for the young but not for those who are older and wiser. Thus, it is expected that as young people reach the magical age of thirty, if not before, they will suddenly see the light, settle down to a home and family in the suburbs, and—faced with the real world—give up their nice but unrealistic values. Thus, a United States Senator told a graduating class with some glee, "Welcome to the establishment." Adults, in fact, get very upset with someone over thirty who professes the values of the counter-culture. Talk-show hosts put such persons down with stinging cracks like "You're thirty-four, aren't you?" which is to say, "You sure look silly trying to be young. Grow up and be like me."

This is an especially crucial problem for the present youth movement. Most of its key figures are now over thirty or approaching that mark. The Chicago Eight defendants, the Beatles, the Rolling Stones, the former civil rights workers, etc., are all technically moving out of the youth category. These people boldly attempt to retain their counter-culture orientation despite society's demand that they grow up. Thus Jerry Rubin shouts, "Don't trust anyone over forty," and notes that anyone with long hair and a beard can pass as young. Despite this, however, the problems faced by members of the counter-culture as they grow older, are obvious. How the older members of the counter-culture deal with this problem may well be the crucial factor in whether or not the youth movements lead to any meaningful change.

The Transition of America

Because of the transitory and unstable nature of generational groups, the changes they are usually able to bring about are in the cultural rather than the economic sphere or the political system (Bottomore, 1969, pp. 104–105). If the cultural change consists only of changes in clothing, hairstyles, speech, and the like, the movement will have no real impact. However, if it leads to changes in values toward work, authority, and the like, the cultural changes might eventually lead to political or economic changes.

As they have grown older, some members of the counter-culture have retained their link to that culture by staying in the academic world. At present, faculties of universities throughout the country have several younger members whose value-systems are often quite different from those of the senior faculty. They do not value professionalism, careerism, and success nearly as much as their colleagues. They do not worry about "the lowering of standards" if students gain more power in the university or if universities go to open admissions. Professional associations such as the American Sociological Association, American Psychological Association, and the American Political Science Association, have had their meetings disrupted by groups of "Young Turks" pressing for change.

It is probable that some former members of the youth movement will be able to find niches within society in which they will be associating with others who will provide them with a reference group for their radical values and possibly even for continued action. Those who remain in the universities clearly have a better chance of doing this than do those who are employed in other institutions. The youth culture is still based in the universities, and organizations such as the New Universities Conference are being formed by former members of the youth movement as they become graduate students and faculty members. NUC and similar organizations, such as the pediatric collective at Lincoln Hospital in New York, Science for People in Boston, the League of Revolutionary Black Workers in Detroit, and the National Welfare Rights Organization, provide bases for older members of the movement (Krause, 1971). To some extent, organizations such as these provide new reference groups for those who, with the years, have grown out of the youth culture. However, only the most committed members of the movement are likely to wind up in such groups; the larger numbers of marginal youth who perhaps had radical ideals while in the crucible of the university are likely to wind up associated mainly with "straight" members of society after leaving college.

Some former student members of the counter-culture have returned after graduation to the "youth ghettos" that now surround many colleges. Since these provide a territorial base for the movement, it may be useful to look at them.

American society is becoming characterized by age segregation in living areas. There are, of course, retirement communities for the old. There are apartment houses which have a minimum age requirement of fifty-five. There are an increasing number of apartment houses for "swinging singles" and young marrieds in the twenty-five-to-thirty-five age-bracket. This type of age-segregation will probably increase in the future and could affect the lifestyles of different age-groups.

Young people with a counter-culture orientation—students, nonstudents, street people, and so forth—are clustering in areas around major universities. This raises the question of what happens when groups that adhere to a cultural system different from that of the dominant society cluster in a territory.

Rubenstein (1970) has presented an interesting analysis of the actions of groups in American history that it may be helpful to review here. It may then be possible to draw some conclusions about the probable future of the youth culture in America.

American independence was followed by a series of Indian revolts, which were vain attempts to resist the expansion of white settlement to territory west of the Mississippi. This continued later in the Far West. Rubenstein notes that these were essentially armed insurrections by domestic groups denied self-determination. The U.S. Army spent the first century of its existence suppressing Indian revolts.

From 1740 to the 1790s, there was a series of revolts by Appalachian debtor-farmers in the western regions of the coastal states, among them Shay's Rebellion (Massachusetts) and the Whisky Rebellion (Pennsylvania). These farmers protested economic, political, and social exploitation by the East Coast. Their protests were characterized by civil disobedience, attacks on officials, and the closing of courts to prevent mortgage foreclosures. Once again, military force was used to control the rebellion.

During the Revolutionary Period, American insurgents resorted to political violence, and the authorities resorted to repression. Civil disobedience, boycotts, rioting, and terrorist attacks were common. The insurgents found themselves pitted against other Americans who supported the British.

The case of the Civil War is well known; this was followed by guerrilla warfare in the postwar South. The South was treated as occupied territory. Terrorist groups engaged in guerrilla warfare in an attempt to drive out the occupying forces. Faced with this, the North eventually returned white supremacy, and President Hayes withdrew Northern troops in 1876.

During the wave of immigration to America, immigrant groups suffered violence at the hands of native Americans. There were anti-Irish riots on the East Coast and mob violence against the Chinese and Japanese on the West Coast. The newer immigrants formed street gangs to protect themselves. There was then and has continued to be continual strife between the working class and the underclass.

There were 250 abortive black insurrections during the years of slavery. After the Civil War, whites often massacred blacks. Following World War I, whites and blacks often battled each other for the control of territory in large cities. The most recent

race riots have been against white-owned property and the police.

Then, in the 1960s, the students revolted. This revolt, as we
have seen, challenged not just political and economic power but
the existing cultural values in the country.

Rubenstein points out that none of these group revolts has
been revolutionary in the sense of attacking central power.
Mass domestic violence has usually been a result of the attempts of out-groups in American society to drive central
power out of their territory and to be able to control their own
affairs. Large, culturally cohesive groups that saw themselves as
controlled by the larger society have continually demanded independence and self-determination. Essentially, these groups
were seeking de facto control of their local territory. Central
power has generally not been threatened at its source; rather,
its representatives have been driven from out-group territory.
The ideology of these groups usually defines the group seeking
autonomy and attempts to increase its internal cohesion and
consciousness rather than emphasizing the overthrow of the existing order.

Rubenstein notes that the prerequisites for this type of revolt
are a high level of group cohesion, usually based on a shared
cultural heritage, and a definable territory that can be claimed
for the group and protected against invasion.

Is the current youth movement developing along these lines?
This is difficult to determine, but we can note some tendencies
in this direction. The cultural cohesion of youth groups is increasing. Legitimizing ideologies are being provided by writers
such as Roszak, Flacks, Reich, and Slater. In areas around
large universities, youth groups are attempting to stake out a
territory they can control. Best known of these is, of course, the
Telegraph Avenue area of Berkeley. There have been a series
of clashes between students and street people on the one side,
and city and university officials and the police on the other.
The largest single clash was during the People's Park battle,

which was clearly a dispute over territory. In the summer of 1970, the city escalated its efforts to keep teenagers and other "freaks" from coming to Berkeley during the annual trek to Mecca by counter-culture-oriented youngsters. There was on the ballot for the April 1971 election a measure supported by the student and black communities that would have provided separate police forces for the black area, the student area, and the "straight" area of the city. Similar communities are developing in Seattle, Madison, Ann Arbor, Boston, and other college areas, although these are not yet as extensive as in Berkeley.

These communities allow dropouts and former college students to maintain their links with the counter-culture. Graduates and those who have finished graduate school often return to the area to work. Thus, counter-culture types with Ph.D.s attempt to get jobs teaching at San Jose State, San Francisco State, Hayward State, and other Bay Area colleges, so that they can live in Berkeley. The most intense conflict between the youth culture and the authorities has been on those campuses that have a radical community both on and off campus.

This still leaves the question whether or not an essentially favored and privileged group can legitimize its protest and transform itself into an out-group. This remains to be seen, but the authorities are already beginning to react to counter-culture types in terms of stereotyped conceptions of the "hippie." "Those freaks" are seen as dirty, smelly, subversive, dope-using criminals (Brown, 1969). This type of reaction on the part of authorities is the sort of thing that can produce a group consciousness on the part of an out-group. There are, in addition, the efforts of the present vice president of the United States, who is probably the best friend the movement ever had. His increasing attacks and reading from the dictionary have produced a consciousness that might have been slower to develop without them.

While it is difficult to draw a firm conclusion about the possibilities of the counter-culture's developing true out-group status in the United States, I would tentatively conclude that this is happening. There is likely to be additional clashes with the representatives of central authority in the youth ghettos of the country and an increasing attempt to gain autonomy within these areas.

If the adherents of the counter-culture do become an out-group in the sense that Rubenstein refers to out-groups, this still suggests that the main thrust of the counter-culture will be to gain control over its own territory. Under what conditions would we expect that drives for local autonomy on the part of out-groups require a rapid transformation of the entire social system?

Rubenstein (1970, p. 167) suggests that this will occur under the following conditions:

1. When those defining themselves as a group are so numerous, in control of such a large geographical area, and so nation-conscious as to attempt secession with some success.
2. When a single group excluded from power at all levels attempts to force a system transformation by resort to "aggressive" violence outside rebel territory.
3. When similarly situated groups conducting separate revolts join forces for the purpose of gaining power simultaneously through radical change in the political system.

The first condition doesn't exist at the moment in the United States. The second condition appears to be developing to some extent, but it is not clear that this will lead to any meaningful change in the system. The third condition presents a distinct possibility, but there are also some problems.

Rubenstein notes that under the third condition, groups usually go through a process of (a) cooperation with other groups for moderate reform, (b) disillusionment and withdrawal from coalitions and formation of group consciousness, and (c) cooperation with carefully selected groups in and out of power as part of a broader strategy for radical change (1970, p. 177).

The racial minorities and underclass out-groups in America appear to have gone through the first two of these steps and are groping around for a way to enter the third.

There are some real prospects and some real problems here. It is possible that blacks, Chicanos, American Indians, Appalachian whites, and counter-culture youth could form this type of alliance through their individual drives for local autonomy. However, the racial minorities have had difficulty getting together and have often accused each other of racism. Poor whites have not shown much sign of readiness to ally themselves with racial minorities, although the development of such groups as the White Panthers suggests that younger members of this group may be starting this process. An additional problem enters when any of these groups attempts to ally with counter-culture youth. The underclass groups are still essentially trying to become part of and reap the benefits of the industrial state, while affluent youth are trying to get out of the industrial system. The goals of economically deprived groups are necessarily different from those of affluent whites.

Still, attempts have been made to form alliances, sometimes showing some success and other times collapsing. The Black Panthers have been most prominent in attempting to form alliances with other underclass groups and the white counter-culture, although the Panthers currently appear to be disintegrating. Groups such as the White Panthers, Young Lords, etc., have modeled themselves after the Panthers, and Panther leaders such as Eldridge Cleaver, Bobby Seale, and Huey Newton have become the heroes of some young whites. Still, the road to such an alliance seems rocky. It may have its best chance if the various out-groups can define their own self-interest in a way congruent with the interests of other groups.

Areas, such as Berkeley, that have a large population of students, counter-culture-oriented street people, and racial minorities, provide the best opportunities for alliances for political action even if they take the conventional form of attempting to win an election. An example of this is the Spring 1971 Berkeley city elections.

A coalition of street people, students, and blacks banded together under the banner of the April Coalition and ran a slate of four acknowledged radicals for the City Council. Three of the coalition members were elected to the Council and a sympathizer was elected mayor. Since the mayor is a voting member of the Council, the election gave the radical coalition a 4–4 standoff with other members of the Council to elect a ninth member who could give the radicals control of the city government. In the same election, the plan to split the police department into three separate units for the student, black, and middle-class communities was defeated, so the results of the election were somewhat mixed. It is also difficult to assess whether or not any significant changes will result from the election of a radical group to the City Council. The group has promised child-care centers, rent control, and a graduated tax on incomes over $12,000 to replace property and sales taxes. Except for the last, these proposals are not particularly profound, and they certainly don't affect the basic structure of society. However, this election does illustrate the phenomenon of territorial control that Rubenstein discussed. The out-groups did band together to gain some control over events in their own territory and did attempt (even though they failed) to drive out central control with their proposal to split the police department.

Thus, it is difficult to determine at this time how likely is a coalition of out-groups that aims at basic change in the larger society. Since, as Rubenstein points out, changes in the American context come about more through group alliances than through economic class alliances, some sort of alliance of out-groups is probably necessary if their protests are going to lead to any meaningful change in the larger social system. Further, there is some question as to whether any *basic* change in the structure of modern societies is possible without some support from the working class. At present, in American society, this type of support is highly unlikely since the workers are often the strongest supporters of the status quo. Of course, it is always possible that circumstances such as a serious economic crisis may bring about a change in the worldview of the working class. It is difficult to determine, however, whether such conditions will come about, and if they do, whether workers will be attracted to a leftwing or rightwing movement under crisis conditions.

In general, youth movements by themselves are unlikely to bring about *basic* changes in modern societies. However, they may provide examples of changes that other segments of society might emulate.

Bottomore (1969, p. 104) stresses some factors which are important in determining whether current protest will lead to any real change. First, student protests have given rise to new relationships and new forms of self-government. These may provide examples to other spheres of society, particularly if students can carry the social attitudes they have formed in the radical movement with them into future occupations. Second, the movement must find some basis in society less ephemeral and confined than the present protest movements. Bottomore notes that students are a small minority in society, and although they can initiate a radical movement, they are not able to continue it alone or to lead it. Social groups who want to alter their conditions of life must find in the doctrines an explanation of their troubles and a guide to effective actions. Third, there must be a clearly articulated theory, something which is presently lacking. Broad social aims are not sufficient. There must be direct efforts which are consistent toward a more desirable way of life. These ideas must be rooted in the actual experience of new types of social organization and elaborated in practical form. Finally, "For the student movement in the USA to become an enduring radical force it would be necessary that the present radicalism should be handed on intact to each new generation of students over a fairly long period of time, and that students after leaving the university, could be inducted into other radical movements which, however, do not exist" (Bottomore, 1969, p. 104).

What conclusions can we reach about the relation of present-day youth movements to social change and the probability of a transition to another form of social system? I think we can say that a transition is occurring and that the counter-culture is a reflection of this but that the counter-culture primarily represents an attempt to develop legitimizing ideologies and value-systems for a changing technological and ecological condition. That is, earlier, I looked at the process through which the value-system of industrial capitalism emerged along with a change in technology. The disintegration of that value-system also is linked to a change in technology.

The objectification and reification of the value-system associated with the emergence of capitalist activity served to legitimize the Industrial Revolution, when in England at the end of the eighteenth century, and on the Continent in the first years of the nineteenth, the invention of machinery and the application of steam to manufacturing, created the surplus necessary for the further elaboration of the division of labor. The phenomenon of the twelfth century in Western Europe was reproduced with greater intensity (Karp and Kelly, 1971b).

If the Industrial Revolution was based on the combination of the *power of the machine with the skill of the human being,* then, as Robert Theobald suggests, "we have now entered a new revolutionary era in which the *power of the machine is combined with the skill of the machine* to form a productive system of, in effect, unlimited capacity. The basis of this new revolution is a greatly increased understanding of the processes of communication between man and machines and between machines themselves, and the change can therefore justly be called the cybernetic revolution." (Theobald, 1963)

On the basis of an analysis of our cybernetic potential, Theobald further suggests:

The evidence is overwhelming. The United States and the other rich countries will shortly have the technological capability to install a productive system based primarily on *machine* power and *machine* skills within the next two decades; market forces will compel both government and business to use cybernated equipment. Since the beginning of the industrial revolution we have witnessed a growing replacement of manpower by machine power, but man's skills were still essential to the utilization of machine power. The coming replacement of man's skills by the machine's skills will destroy many jobs and render useless the work experience of vast numbers now employed. The possibility of obtaining employment in one of the restricted number of new fields will depend to a very large extent on the level of skill and education of the job applicant. It follows that the decline in job opportunities will be most severe for those who perform repetitive tasks and whose work can most easily be done by machines. This conclusion implies the *complete* breakdown of our present socioeconomic system, which depends on the ability to provide jobs for all who require them. The resulting situation is paradoxical. We are going to be able to produce more goods than ever before and we therefore have the ability to provide a standard of living compatible with the maintenance of human dignity for everybody. However, because we still believe that the income levels of the vast majority of the population should depend on their ability to continue working, over 20 percent of the American population is exiled from the abundant economy and this percentage will grow, rather than decline, in coming years.

We are trapped by "the dismal science"—economics. The founders of economic theory believed that we could *never* achieve abundance and therefore defined economics as the art of "distributing scarce resources." Today we already have large-scale agricultural surpluses and we have the ability to produce more than $60 billion in additional goods and services with our *presently* existing productive capacity; it is therefore ludicrous to continue to define economics as the art of distributing scarce resources. . . . Abundance has arrived. [Theobald, 1963].

From an ecological perspective, ways of life are a product of conditions of life. As ecological conditions change, patterns of behavior will change and the legitimizing ideologies and central value-systems will also change. This is not because technological change causes cultural changes. The process is more involved and does not involve a simple cause-effect relationship. Through externalization, human beings create both technology and social reality. Once created, both of these act back on their creators and change the environment in which men live. The physical environment is changed as new technology is invented, the social environment is changed as worldviews are altered. This is a continual process that occurs as human beings seek to make sense of the world in which they live. Social movements represent collective attempts to define and make sense of the world. They are neither "caused" by technological change nor do they "cause" such change. Rather, the continual change is a process which flows both ways.

I have tried to show earlier that the behavior and value system associated with it, referred to as counter-culture, derives from the particular position of middle-class youth in American society. The enormous technological progress that has occurred since the Industrial Revolution has produced a world of abundance for those who are located in the middle class or above. The present generation of middle-class youth is the first large group to be raised entirely in a world of abundance. Further, it is the first large group of persons to be released from the labor market for a significant period of their lives. That is, the college youth population experiences an ecological condition for which men have been striving for ages: one of abundance that is not dependent upon their own labor.

Further, those students who have been most active in the political wing of the youth movement tend to be the offspring of those members of the middle class who are oriented toward liberal or humanistic values and who advocated and built the welfare state. The present generation was born into that welfare state and has experienced it as a reality rather than a hypothetical event. They thus are likely to extend the value-system they received from their parents and to build a critique of the welfare state from that value-system.

This is important because it gets to the heart of the transition going on with regard to the culture of industrial capitalism. The spirit of capitalism developed over a long period of time and was related to technological changes, especially in the latter stages of its development during the Industrial Revolution. The erosion of the value-system of capitalism has also been occurring slowly over a long period of time. The rise of large productive organizations based on expensive machinery, the corporate form of organization which goes with this, the increased role of government in the economy, and the rise of the welfare state have all chipped away at that value-system. Still, these changes were mainly oriented to patching up the existing economic system, and indeed, patching up the ideological justifications which went with it. The present generation of college youth is merely carrying that process a little further and is getting close to asking questions about the underlying assumptions on which the entire ideological chain is built.

A revolution, in the sense of a basic change in both power relations and in the culture of a society, takes place over several generations. It is not until an existing social reality has been chipped away at for some time that a relatively large number of persons will start asking questions about the basic assumptions on which an entire system is built. A great deal of groundwork is necessary before a new form of organization is ready to emerge. One thing is clear in those who are oriented toward the youthful counter-culture: they are less likely to see the idea of socialism and the values that are associated with it as an absolute evil. Some have even come to see the value-system of capitalism in that light.

Can we then conclude that the present generation will bring about a transition in the basic form of American society as its members reach positions of power? I think not. There are two basic reasons why I think it is still too soon for a full transformation to take place. The first of these relates to the fact that the humanistic youth with which we have been mainly concerned in this book are still only a minority of their particular age-group. We must keep in mind that at least half of the eighteen-year-olds in the United States do not go to college, and we have seen that the value-system of this group is quite different from that of college youth. Further, not all—or even a majority—of college youth are oriented toward the counter-culture value-system. It is mainly those students at relatively "good" schools, and those who major in the humanities and the social sciences, who are oriented this way. The counter-culture value-system is spreading among this age group, but it has not yet swept the day. In addition, the particular condition of being affluent and not in the labor force holds only until students leave the university, and as I suggested earlier, while those who are near the core of the alternative value-system may be able to retain that orientation, the more marginal students probably won't be able to.

As I noted earlier, the gap is not strictly generational, although it is correlated with generational phenomena. As the humanistic youth grow older, they will find that they are fighting not so much the older generation but rather their age peers, who are oriented toward the value-system of industrial capitalism.

To state that a full transformation is not likely to occur during the lifespan of this generation does not mean that a transition is not in progress nor that the society will continue to be the same. The erosion of the value-system of industrial capitalism, which has been occurring slowly for some time now, will continue, probably at an accelerated pace. The expansion of education, the questions raised by the environmental crisis, the increased exposure to alternative realities that is available through mass communication, travel, and education, and the expansion of the social sciences, will all contribute to this process.

112

It will probably be the next generation that gets to the root assumptions of our culture. This, of course, will not happen in a vacuum. Continued changes in institutions and values will set the stage for the issues likely to concern that generation. And, as in the present situation, the issues that are raised will not be strictly a generational phenomenon.

The rate at which all this occurs will probably be affected a great deal by the degree to which more people are removed from the labor market for long periods of time, with the corresponding leisure to delve into questions about self-actualization, basic human needs, and the degree to which scarcity is overcome physically and in terms of the cultural definitions of scarcity. To the extent that abundance and the conditions associated with it do arrive, a society oriented toward human needs will evolve.

I am contending that the present youthful dissent is related to an ongoing process of changes in technology and social reality that is leading to the breakdown of the values and authority of industrial capitalism. Through a rather slow process of definition, I think an ideology and a general vision of future society is developing. As I indicated earlier, that vision will be put into practice only if youth groups can form viable coalitions with other out-groups in this society, and also with those intellectuals and liberals who are oriented toward humanistic values but are reluctant to challenge the basic assumptions of their society. Since it is difficult to predict whether such an alliance will develop, I will not predict whether that future vision will ever become reality. However, I will attempt to delineate the vision of that future that I think is developing and to show how some of the changes that reflect a continuing erosion of the culture of industrial capitalism might occur.

NINE

The Human Society: The Social Construction of an Alternative Reality

Predicting the future is, at best, a precarious enterprise. This is especially so if one is attempting to do so as part of a sociological analysis. Nevertheless, if one proceeds with caution, the effort can be quite worthwhile. If nothing else, it provides an opportunity to test the validity of an analysis by seeing how closely it fits what actually happens. More important, perhaps, a vision of the future can provide a model or goal for a society as it evolves. At any rate, the analysis of youth movements in this book suggests that some sort of transition is about to occur in industrial societies, and the analysis would not be complete without some attempt to show where that transition might lead.

Having decided to analyze the present trends in industrial societies, one might be concerned with what to call a postindustrial society. The term "postindustrial" itself was coined to refer to a society in which less than half the labor force was engaged in industrial production; that is, a society based on tertiary employment. Since we are already in such a society, this term is not too useful in describing the future.

Various writers have coined terms to designate the society into which they think we are moving. Among the terms suggested are: technetronic society, electric age, cybernetic society, and superindustrial society. These terms either emphasize some particular technological development or suggest that the future will be a bigger, more glorious version of the past. Since I have been implying throughout this analysis that the present state of ecological development in advanced industrial societies allows the possibility of a society based on the fulfillment of human needs to develop, I prefer to use a term that implies this. Thus, I will simply call the post-transition society the "human society." While this is a simple term, it implies a lot. A society based on human needs rather than production, consumption, expansion, and the like, would certainly be quite different from our present system. Although it is possible that the ecological base might not change too much, the institutional arrangements built upon that base might change quite a lot. With this in mind, we can proceed to an analysis of the human society and how it might develop.

In developing this analysis, I have drawn on three types of data. First, I have used sociological analyses of present trends in various institutions. Here the biggest problem is that one can't always be sure that a particular trend will continue without reversing itself or changing into something else. However, I think there are some trends which would be consistent with the ecological changes that I believe are occurring.

Several writers, among them social scientists as well as others, have suggested alterations in our present institutions that they feel might be more consonant with human needs than our present arrangements. These suggestions provide a second source of ideas about what the future might look like. We, of course, have to be careful in accepting any particular idea. It should, in general, be consistent with other trends and not totally someone's pipe dream. That is, there should be some possibility that the suggestion might be adopted and could work within the framework of the total society.

A third source of data comes from the youth movements

themselves. If present youth movements represent an attempt to adjust to changing ecological conditions, the content of those movements should suggest something about the type of society that will result after the transition period. Accordingly, I have examined the youth movements for institutional arrangements that might occur on a larger scale in the future.

Putting these diverse ideas together is no easy matter. The important thing is to look for ways in which changes in one institution would be consistent with changes in another institution, since there is a general tendency for institutions to hang together. Any particular institution must provide some support for others with which it is linked. This is mainly because of the human need for cognitive consistency. As human beings act out the patterns of behavior that make up institutions, there must be some consistency in the form of these institutions. An orientation learned one place generally has an application elsewhere. Thus, if the Protestant Ethic and the spirit of capitalism go together, a change in the economic institution might well be accompanied by a change in the religious institution. With this in mind, we can now begin to outline the forms of some of the institutions of the future society.

The Economic System

Probably the central institution in any society is the economic one. It might not determine everything else, but it certainly puts powerful constraints on the form of other institutions. It, therefore, seems that we should start this analysis with the economic institution. Here we run into an immediate problem. The economic arrangements of a mature industrial society are exceedingly complex and interlocking. Any major change in the economic structure of a corporate welfare state might disrupt it so badly that the ecological base on which we wish to build might be destroyed. Does this mean, then, that no major change in society is likely to occur unless the present economic structure is ripped down and we return to some pastoral past? Either a continuation of the present system, or a return to some preindustrial state, would clearly not be consistent with the analysis of this book. If we are to maintain the present base and yet build a human society on it, it is necessary to find a way to allow activities to be performed for something other than extrinsic rewards. The alteration that might permit this is the guaranteed income.

During the last decade, a debate has been brewing about the guaranteed-income proposals put forth by Friedman (1962) and Theobald (1963). The GMI has been called an extreme left-wing plan, a restatement of New Deal philosophy, a mainstream liberal plan, and a conservative or reactionary proposal. Most of this confusion results because there are several different goals which can be stressed in presenting a GMI proposal, and different proponents have stressed different goals. Thus, in order to understand the nature of the GMI and why it is important to our analysis of the development of a human society, it is necessary to look at the goals that proponents have in mind when they make these proposals.

Being an economic conservative (or nineteenth-century liberal), Friedman (1962) sees most of the economic problems of the country as a result of government interference in the economy, especially through the welfare state. At the same time, he recognizes that no civilized society can have people starving in the streets. He notes that the main problem that the poor have is that they have no money. Consequently, he proposes a negative income tax (guaranteed income) as a means of providing for the poor and, at the same time, beginning to dismantle the welfare state. Essentially, Friedman's proposal represents a low-level dole to the poor, which would be linked with such things as the elimination of public housing, the elimination of public education (to be replaced by a system of vouchers which could be used at the private school of one's choice), the private ownership of the national parks, etc. Since most of Friedman's proposal represents an attempt to return to the past, it is not too important in our analysis of the future. The important aspects are the suggestion that the only criteria for receiving the guaranteed income would be need and that the program would be administered through the Internal Revenue Service. Although Friedman is proposing an end to government interference in the economy, his plan still is perceived as radical by most conservatives and was roundly denounced by the *National Review*.

A second goal of the guaranteed income is proposed by several twentieth-century liberals, such as Keyserling (1967) and Tobin (1967). Their emphasis is on changing the welfare system and eliminating poverty. They note that about 40 percent of all poverty in the United States is suffered by those who are not or should not be within the employment stream. These include such groups as women, the aged, and the blind. They note several problems with the present welfare system that they feel can only be eliminated by a complete change of the system.

The problems of the present welfare system are of four kinds (Tobin, 1967). First, there is inadequate coverage. The vast majority of poor households in the United States receive no public assistance, due to the fact that the working poor and able-bodied adults are not eligible, and due to residence requirements. There has been some attempt recently to deal with this problem in a patchwork way, but it still persists.

A second problem is one of inadequate benefits. Although the Federal Government pays 60 percent of AFDC, most states do not meet their own standards of a minimum budget. Further, the wide discrepancy in payments between states is grossly unfair and accentuates migration from the southern states into the urban ghettos of the North.

Third, most welfare programs are characterized by perverse incentives. Since benefits are reduced dollar for dollar on earnings, the poor can't gain anything by working unless they can earn more than the maximum welfare payments.

Fourth, the present system is characterized by excessive administration. Since the means test to prevent cheating is the dominating concern of the system, there is petty surveillance over the details of a recipient's expenditures and life. This destroys the self-concepts of the poor, and through a self-fulfilling prophecy, leads them to remain dependent. In addition, the excessive administration is very expensive and leads to a good share of poverty funds being used to keep the welfare bureaucracy going rather than meeting the needs of the poor.

To deal with these problems, a guaranteed income is proposed. This would provide a floor under the incomes of everyone and would be financed by the Federal Government in order to provide a uniform national standard. Since it would be based on need, it would allow the working poor to be eligible.

Basically, a guaranteed income plan contains three elements: a guaranteed minimum income line, which would be the floor below which no one could fall; a break-even point, at which the Government would stop paying the negative income tax; and a negative tax rate. The recipient would be paid the difference between his income and the break-even point after this difference is multiplied by the negative tax rate. Thus, if the break-even point were set at $3200 for a family of four and the family had no income, it would receive $3200 if the negative tax rate was 100% and would receive $1600 if the tax rate was 50%. In the latter case, the $1600 would be the GMI line. If the negative tax rate is 100%, the recipient always reaches the break-even point. If the tax rate is less than 100%, the recipient always gains by working. Thus, the proposal contains a built-in incentive to work. If the recipient earns $1000, and the negative tax rate is 50%, he receives 50% of $2200 and this $1100 plus the $1000 he earned gives him a total income of $2100, which is of course more than the $1600 received by the man who does not work.

The GMI, as proposed under the second goal, would be financed from money in the present welfare system, from economic expansion, and from monies taken from other sources, such as defense spending.

Recently, a version of the guaranteed income was proposed by the President under the name Family Assistance Plan. The FAP plan would essentially set the GMI line at $1600, the tax rate at 50%, and the break-even point at $3200, which is what Friedman originally proposed. FAP is not a true guaranteed income, however. While it does provide a Federal floor under incomes, thus guaranteeing a minimum income regardless of residence, and while it does provide for payments for the working poor, it contains a work requirement since the Administration didn't have sufficient confidence in the built-in work-incentive. In order to qualify for FAP, a person must register for and accept whatever work is available. Further, the FAP proposal keeps the power to disperse funds in the hands of local officials, where it can be used as a control mechanism.

At this point, it is uncertain whether the FAP program will be approved by Congress, or if it is, exactly what it will finally look like. It is significant, however, in indicating how far the idea of a guaranteed income—which only a few years ago was considered a far-out radical plan—has come, since a watered-down version of it has been proposed by a conservative President. While even the FAP plan is considered too radical by some, it is being discussed, and there is much opposition to it on the ground that it is too conservative.

Despite the differences between the GMI proposal of Friedman, that of the liberals, and the FAP plan, they are all similar in an important respect. They all retain as a primary economic goal the idea of full employment maintained by economic growth. Thus, these proposals do not advocate any basic change in the goals of the society and do not provide any basis for the human society that I am attempting to analyze. To provide this basis, it is necessary to look at some further goals of the guaranteed income.

The GMI plan proposed by Theobald (1963), while it accepts the first two goals discussed above, departs radically from the other proposals by including additional goals. Theobald sees the GMI as a way to break the link between jobs and incomes and establish new principles to deal with cybernation (the combination of mechanized machinery, computers, and the science of cybernetics). The basic principle of this proposal is that each individual has a right to a minimal share of the production of the society. This would be a constitutional right and would apply to all citizens without exception. It can be seen that this would be a significant departure from our current way of looking at the world.

The notion of a job as an activity separated from other activities of life, is largely characteristic of modern industrial societies. As I noted earlier, in the United States work has become an almost irreplaceable element in establishing a sense of worth. This has led to the notion that leisure is that time when one is not working and has led to the process (described earlier) through which all activity is transformed intó labor work performed for extrinsic rewards. The notion of the importance of work developed when the most urgent need of the socioeconomic system was defined in terms of an increase in production. As I noted earlier, past patterns of thought become reified in the present patterns of institutions and, thus, remain long after they have any meaning. That is, there is nothing sacred about organizing human activities into "jobs" for which wages are paid. This is merely the way things are done in the era of industrial capitalism.

What Theobald is challenging, then, is the unrecognized underlying assumption that it is necessary for every person to "work" in the sense of holding a "job" even in a highly automated society. He is challenging this both on the grounds that it will no longer be possible to provide jobs for everyone as service jobs, white-collar jobs, and middle-management jobs become automated, and more important, on the grounds that it is *undesirable* to maintain full employment even if we could invent enough jobs to do so. He is suggesting that there may be better ways to ensure that the necessary work in a society is performed.

The heart of the Keynesian analysis of the economic systems of industrial societies is that it is possible to produce an excess supply of goods. Consequently, demand must be kept high to create jobs to provide funds to consume this supply of goods, and this ability to consume will produce more demand, thereby creating more jobs, etc. (A great deal of government spending, especially on war and related activities, helps this process and is probably essentially to it.) Noting that this is a vicious circle which seems to be running for its own sake, Theobald asks why we must keep running in this circle. Why, indeed? And, if it is not necessary to keep the circle going, then the best way to break it is to provide another source for the right to consume besides jobholding. So one of Theobald's goals is to break the link between jobs and income, both because it will probably be necessary to do so and because it is desirable to do so.

The implementation of a guaranteed income would then eliminate the need for forced economic growth and allow the society to begin dealing with another goal: that of saving the environment. Saving the environment involves more than merely treating some symptoms of the problem, such as air pollution, water pollution, soil erosion, and the like. It involves looking at the source of the problems, which is the continued expansion of the economic system and increased population.

There is a tendency to view the problem of overpopulation as one that characterizes only underdeveloped or preindustrial societies. Thus, we worry about overpopulation in India and China but assume that it is not a serious problem in the United States. However, if we define the problem of overpopulation in terms of the environment, we might reach quite different conclusions.

In environmental terms, "most overpopulated is that nation whose people by virtue of their numbers and their activities are most rapidly decreasing the ability of the land to support human life" (Davis, 1970). On this basis, it is not just the number of people in an area that determines the effect of population on the environment, but rather the number of people multiplied by a factor that represents the standard of living of the population. Thus, an advanced economic society provides a standard of living that affects the environment far more than an underdeveloped nation. It is estimated that one American has an effect on the environment at least twenty-five times that of one Indian. Looked at this way, the American population has the same affect upon the environment as would four billion Indians.

An economy based upon the Keynesian concept of continued growth in population and productivity could continue to work only if the earth and its resources were expanding at an annual rate of 4 to 5 percent. One cannot expand indefinitely in a finite world.

Our measure of economic well-being reflects the way we look at the world. The gross national product (an appropriate name) measures only the amount of economic activity. It says nothing about the quality of that activity and gives a plus value to any economic activity even if it involves the destruction of a river or otherwise decreases the quality of life. A human society would need a different measure of economic well-being.

By breaking the link between jobs and incomes, the guaranteed income would allow us to end forced economic growth and begin saving the environment. It would not accomplish this by itself, of course. Also needed would be a commitment to zero population growth accomplished by such means as legalized abortion subsidized by the government, changing the tax structure so as not to reward people for having children, and alerting the people to the serious nature of the environmental problem. As in its other goals, the guaranteed income only provides a means to an end; it does not in itself assure that end. We should keep this in mind when examining the GMI proposals.

The exact effect the GMI would have depends on how it is used in conjunction with basic changes in values.

There is an additional goal of the guaranteed income which, when combined with the ones mentioned above, indicates some of the possibilities of a human society. The GMI is intended to increase individual freedom and allow the development of a pluralistic society. By establishing a second means of distributing the right to consume, the GMI would increase the freedom to dissent and to make one's own decisions. Since a person would have the choice of working to earn more than the guaranteed income, or living at the GMI level and engaging in other activities, he would not be totally dependent on an employer, as he is now. Jefferson noted that no man was truly free who had to work for another. We should emphasize that, at least at first, most people would continue to work because they would prefer to live above the GMI line, but the possibility of developing alternative lifestyles would increase. Of course, the society would have to develop a tolerance for alternative lifestyles that it does not presently have.

There are any number of activities in which men could engage if they were not occupied with labor work. Leisure work is that done for its own sake and is activity in which one is totally involved. Immediately, one can picture activities such as writing poetry, painting, making music, and other artistic activities. However, everyone wouldn't be inclined toward this sort of activity, and there are plenty of other things that people enjoy doing. Some of these might well be the same things people now do as labor work, only the activity would have a different character if done as leisure. Theobald (1963) suggests that consentives (groups of persons voluntarily joining together to produce consumer goods) might arise. These would be nonprofit enterprises that might exist at the same time as did marketives (profitmaking enterprises). Persons on a guaranteed income would be able to live at a decent level without making profit if they so choose.

What is the likelihood that a guaranteed income that would permit this kind of freedom and diversity, might be adopted in the United States? It is clear that there would be a great deal of opposition to such an idea, but there are also some favorable aspects. Arensberg (in Theobald, 1965) has noted that new cultural innovations are most likely to be accepted when they can be fitted into already existing ways, when they can be set in terms culturally acceptable to those who must use them. Studies of comparative cultural and institutional evolution suggest that the effects of a successfully adaptive innovation in a social system are twofold: 1) to hold on to something tried and true and conserve the old in the face of change and 2) the opening of a vast new door permitting a "splendid serendipity." Evolutionary advance is at least a two-step process. It is conservative and trailblazing at once and in that order.

The GMI would fit this type of two-step process. It would preserve and restore the free market, leave unchanged the idea of private property, retain the freedom of persons to choose their work and make as much money as they could. At the same time, it would permit some persons to attempt all sorts of innovations that, over time, might greatly change the society. That is, while it would permit the present patterns of behavior to continue, it would remove some of the restrictions on developing new ones.

While the FAP proposal of the Nixon Administration is a long way from the type of GMI Theobald proposes, the fact that even this is being considered shows that attitudes are beginning to change. Several heads of large corporations have endorsed the idea of a guaranteed income as a welfare measure, recognizing that this would allow a larger number of people to become consumers and would be good for business. If a guaranteed income is adopted with the short-range goals of preserving the present system in mind, it might not be nearly as difficult to use it the way Theobald advocates.

Since many conservatives are frightened even by the FAP

proposal, it might be politically expedient to emphasize the short-run effects of a guaranteed income and not scare people with discussions of a freewheeling, pluralistic society, which some might see as anarchy. However, as Theobald notes, all significant actions necessarily have both favorable and unfavorable consequences. We need to maximize the favorable consequences and can only do this if we are fully aware of what is likely to happen with the adoption of a GMI.

In order to keep the GMI from being used as a control mechanism by a powerful central government, the funds would have to be provided as an absolute constitutional right which could not be taken away under any circumstances. There would, of course, be no means test or other pseudo-sympathetic control device. Since funds would be provided directly to the people without intervening agencies and could be used in any way the people desired, it might be possible to tie the demand for a GMI to the demand for local autonomy for culturally diverse groups. This might be one sort of issue on which many of the American out-groups could form a coalition for political action.

The very long range goal of the GMI is full unemployment. It is seen as the initial point of leverage in changing from an industrial era to the human era. The GMI is essentially a transition device designed to allow revolutionary changes to occur in an evolutionary matter. As such, it could be the key to a change to a human society, provided that it could ever be accepted and provided that it were used properly. It could, at least in the near future, work within the context of capitalism but, as noted below, would eventually require a change to socialism in order to be effective.

There is some question as to how many people from today's population could handle the freedom of choice that they would obtain under a guaranteed income. It is, of course, possible that most people would be totally lost without the job mechanism keeping them under control and that we would wind up with large numbers of drug users or persons engaged in other means of escape. While it is true that most of the present population would probably have difficulty handling this type of freedom, that is not very relevant. The way human beings behave in one historical period under one form of social organization does not tell us much about how they will behave at another point in history under different conditions. What is important is whether a population raised in a society whose institutions were set up to prepare people for true freedom, instead of for taking orders, would be able to handle this freedom.

We now have, in the youth movements, large numbers of people who don't have their identities wrapped up in occupations and who seem able to develop identities based on other factors. There is nothing inherent about the need for jobs; that is a cultural need that most people have picked up in this society. The youth movements may indicate that a guaranteed income could work quite well. The point is that the GMI only provides the means to be free; it does not ensure that men will properly use those means.

How well men are able to take advantage of the potentials of a GMI probably depends upon the shape of other institutions in the society, since institutions tend to hang together and the worldview one obtains through education, religion, and in the family will have a potent effect on his ability to be free. Thus, we will now look at the shape other institutions might take in a human society, beginning with education.

Education

Our present educational system developed to meet the needs of an industrializing economy. It is cast in the mold of the factory. Learning is fragmented into disciplines and courses, and certain "subjects" are taught at set times throughout the day. At 9:00 one studies English, at 10:00 he suddenly becomes interested in mathematics, and so on throughout the day. The purpose of the whole system is to train people for their roles as workers and consumers. Probably more important than the specific training one receives to prepare for future jobholding, is the training one receives in being at the right place at the right time, learning to do that which he would rather not do, and learning to follow orders.

The entire educational system rests upon the often unnoticed assumption that learning is uninteresting. Since no one would learn for learning's sake, it is necessary to bribe the learner with a set of extrinsic rewards, most important among them, grades. Grades provide a scarcity-based extrinsic reward system to motivate persons to engage in uninteresting activity. There are only so many good grades to go around, so children learn to compete for them. Of course, as with all extrinsic rewards, the rewards inevitably become more important than the activity itself and become the main concern of the students. Grades hinder communication between teacher and student as well as between student and student; emphasize extrinsics at the cost of real learning; encourage mechanical, trivial learning; make niggers out of students; and put an emphasis on cheating (Robertson and Steele, 1971). In short, they prepare the student for the other institutions that he is likely to enter. This type of educational system meets the needs of the present industrial system by mass-producing thousands of persons who have built up a tolerance for boring activities and have learned that there are "right" answers to questions and that the right answers are the ones that experts give. One does not provide his own answers, for they would be wrong.

There has been an age-old battle over the nature of learning that essentially boils down to the question whether one learns by having information poured into him or whether one's own inner potentialities should be developed. If you are training people for jobs and to take orders, they then must learn what someone else decides is essential for them to learn in order to fit the needs of the economic system. If you are preparing people to make free choices in an open society, a quite different kind of education is called for.

In the last few years, there has been a wave of criticism of our present educational system, most of it emphasizing the deadening affect of an educational system based mainly on the control of the persons within it. The heart of the criticism was contained in the manifesto of the youth movement, Farber's (1969) notorious *The Student as Nigger*. The criticism finally seems to be making an impact, since now such a basically conservative member of the establishment as Silberman (1970) has accepted many of the conclusions of the dissidents.

There is now being advocated a new type of education for the future. (The ideas actually are not new: they have been around at least as far back as the ancient Greeks.) The education of the future, instead of stressing the learning of set subject-matter, will involve students in learning how to learn. This essentially involves the art of learning to ask embarrassing questions (Postman and Weingartner, 1969). Once a person has learned to ask questions—relevant, appropriate, and substantial questions—he has learned how to learn, and no one can keep him from learning whatever he needs to know. The essence of this kind of learning is that the learner learns to question the underlying assumptions of his culture and therefore render social reality transparent. Preparing large numbers of people to do this is risky business for any society, as its fondest beliefs and institutional arrangements are all likely to be questioned and it might appear as though chaos will result. The only kind of society that could afford to do this would be one whose goals are primarily oriented to the satisfaction of human needs.

In this type of free educational environment, learners would follow their natural interests and learn that which was most important to them. If learning is not transformed into labor work through extrinsic rewards, it will be sought as its own end, and a person following his own interests will learn a great deal more than someone being trained in accord with another's interests. Schools from the beginning through the universities would be communities of free learners, none of which would have any power over the others at all.

The exact form that such learning communities might take is unimportant. There have been several diverse suggestions. Probably, a number of different arrangements would be tried simultaneously. There are currently a host of experiments with free universities, free schools, and other arrangements outside the existing system. In addition, some schools within the present system are trying out some of the ideas of free education. For instance, a new state college on the West Coast lists the following as its aims:

This college has collected scholars and experts who, insofar as they inquire in their fields of interest, will by their presence here together form a living link between our present society and the past, a source of power with which to help us all meet the future. Students will work as colleagues with faculty and others, and together these people will *try* (that word is emphasized because it involves all of the college's people in continual change) to create a place whose graduates can as adults be undogmatic citizens and uncomplacently confident individuals in a changing world.

We assume that toward this end the most valuable service (we) can offer is to initiate a process of continuing learning by preparing a student with the methods of learning and experimentation, by encouraging independence in pursuit of inquiries that interest and motivate him, and by providing him with counsel and resources to test this knowledge and ability. Put negatively, we do not intend to stamp a "product" with a brand of a particular academic elite nor of a narrowly conceived vocation.

(Our) task, then, is to begin a process of continuing learning. We should be pleased if our graduate turns out to be a generalist, or one familiar with one of today's great problems, and satisfied if he's a specialist, even a narrow one. Terms like "breadth and depth requirements" will have no place here, since they assume that the B.A. is, on one hand, the end of all education, or, in a few cases, not even the beginning, but simply a prep school for "real" learning later. [McCann, 1970]

As newly opening schools and colleges try these experimental practices, they will serve as models for changes in the older institutions. Since the universities are where the youth movements are strongest, they should be able to press for changes here. The large number of younger faculty members in our colleges also suggest possibilities of change, since many of them are oriented toward the "new" education. The public schools will yield more slowly, but the young teachers now coming out of the universities should be able to effect some changes, and the competitive effect of the free schools combined with the effect of critiques such as the Silberman report should aid this process.

As the present educational system prepares people for a society based on performance of extrinsically rewarded activities performed as jobs, so should a free educational system prepare people to engage in activities performed for their own sake. It should be apparent that changes in the educational system and changes in the economic system will have to evolve together. As long as it is necessary to type, grade, and categorize people for entrance into bureaucratically organized job-activities, there will be some limitation on how "free" the educational system can become. The greater the number of persons who are able to disengage themselves from the job mechanism through a guaranteed income, the greater the possibilities for free education, and vice versa. The evolution of social institutions is a complex, intertwined process, and consists of a changing of the ways in which people interact with each other to create new social realities. This is always an ongoing process, and that is how these institutions will be transformed.

The Family

In many ways, the family is the basic institution in a society. A person's way of interacting in other institutions, his attitude toward authority, and many of his values are shaped first in the family. More important, perhaps, the family is a place where a person can theoretically drop his role pretenses and interact on the basis of his real self. Unfortunately, as I noted earlier, this doesn't happen as often in modern societies as it might. The universal fake-out is carried on in the family as well as outside the family. Consequently, one change that seems necessary in the family is that it again become a place where one can enjoy intimate association.

Intimate association is that relationship between persons in which they reveal themselves in all their weaknesses, dropping the role performances that usually conceal the self. It is through the process of intimate association that a person is able to obtain direct self-acceptance based upon a positive reaction to what he really is, rather than to his public self. It is the type of relationship that characterizes the best marriages and all true friendships. For intimate association to occur, the persons involved must see each other on a fairly regular basis and in an informal setting where they do not have to play their customary roles. Intimate association does not exist unless the two people involved sometimes talk about the ultimate meanings of their lives. Unless people do this to some extent, their relationship will remain superficial.

Most "friendships" do not really involve intimate association, since they do not involve discussion of the ultimate meanings of persons' lives and do not involve the full dropping of role performances that characterize this kind of relationship. At present, most marriages do not fully involve intimate association either.

The process of urbanization and industrialization reduced the size of the family, so that mature industrial societies are characterized by the nuclear family consisting of parents and children only, instead of an extended family involving many relatives. This means that the family at best only provides the opportunity for intimate association with one other adult. At present, two contradictory trends are apparent in family size. One involves a move toward an even smaller family, as there are likely to be more married couples who do not have children. This would be the smallest possible family unit, consisting of only two persons. The opposite trend involves the move toward some sort of communal living, where several adults and whatever children they have form a family unit.

The move toward communal living, especially on the part of the young, represents an attempt to recapture a *Gemeinschaft* where a person can relate to several adults on the basis of intimate association and thereby gain self-acceptance. This new type of extended family is taking many directions and forms. It might involve an almost random collection of individuals. It might involve something as formal as the relationship suggested by Rimmer (1967), in which two or three couples form a corporate marriage in which intimate association is sought by each of the pairs in the group, resulting in group intimate association. In addition, some of these groups might choose to keep sexual relations confined to any particular couples and not have these relationships occurring between the couples. Others might prefer to allow sexual relations between all male-female pairs, feeling that sexual relations are a natural outgrowth of intimate association between opposite-sexed members.

While these "extended" families are likely to take many forms, they generally represent an attempt to reestablish a place where direct self-acceptance can be found. Since the nuclear family appeared as a result of economic changes in industrial societies, it should be clear that communal living will be most possible for those persons who can remain relatively free of the formal labor market. Thus, they are at present mainly a practice of the young. How widespread such arrangements can become in the population at large depends on whether or not some arrangement such as the guaranteed income is adopted. The combination of the GMI and a communal family could provide an economically and psychologically secure base for persons in our human society. Since intimate association, with more than one other person, is essential for human survival, some form of communal living is likely to become institution-alized and accepted in the relatively near future but it is un-likely to become the predominant family form.

Organizational Form

Industrial societies are characterized by the organizational form known as bureaucracy. Bureaucracies are best suited to the performance of repetitive tasks in an unchanging environment. They were probably best suited to the Victorian age, in which they reached their peak efficiency and during which Weber con-cluded that they were the ultimate form of social organization. However, bureaucracy might not be the most efficient form of organization where there is rapid and unexpected change and it is necessary to bring together persons of diverse, highly special-ized competence to deal with some problem. These conditions favor the task force or temporary-adaptive form of organiza-tion.

Bennis and Slater (1963) see the emerging form of social or-ganization to be the temporary-adaptive form. In large organi-zations, this involves task forces organized around problems to be solved by groups of relative strangers with diverse skills. These groups are organic: they evolve in response to a problem rather than to set role expectations. Interaction in such groups involves full and free communication regardless of rank, re-liance on consensus, influence based on competence, an atmo-sphere that permits and encourages emotional expression as well as task orientation, and a basically human bias. This type of organization increases the power and availability of persons not committed to the status quo. Bennis and Slater feel that this form of organization is the only system that can cope with the changing demands of the future world.

It should be apparent that the temporary adaptive form of

organization can work in business, government, education, and less formal groups. It is consistent with the idea of consentives, education that attempts to develop human potential, and a looser, more flexible society.

Since the bureaucratic form of organization integrates diverse roles and provides role expectations which allow persons to interact with each other in accordance with some set of rules, we might ask how persons will be able to interact without these set role expectations. This will require a change in the type of self-concept prevalent in the society.

The Self-Concept

If persons are to interact on an interpersonal basis instead of an interrole basis, they will need some way of predicting each other's behavior. At present, this would involve a long process of breaking down the fronts that they have built to hide themselves before they would know enough about each other to interact in any meaningful way. This process would be less time-consuming if individuals were more like each other than they were different. To assert that persons will become more similar raises the specter of a rather dull society in which everyone is alike. Most of us find this thought unpleasant, at the very least. However, this results because we tend to picture all persons as being like some type of present specialized semiperson. This would indeed be a rather dull society, since many of the aspects of human potential would not be present. Since most aspects are present in any cultural system in some form, I doubt that such a society is even possible.

If we look at the idea of a more uniform population in a different way, however, different conclusions can be reached. What we now do during the process of personality development is to limit the full range of human potential with which each person starts, by learning to play certain roles that combine to form the kind of person an individual is trying to be. Other aspects of the self are denied and often projected onto others. In this way, the individual alienates aspects of his self, which are then seen as characteristics of others. This is accomplished through the process I have called the universal fake-out.

If instead of the present process of personality development, persons were allowed to develop a greater portion of their potential, they would become more alike, since each would represent a wider range of the human potential. There would be less variation between persons, but greater variation within a person. Uniformity, then, could be tolerated only if all people were transformed into full human beings, rather than the specialized roleplayers.

Developing a fuller range of the self would be consistent with an educational system designed to encourage self-expression, a freer economic system, and an extended form of family that allowed the development of direct self-acceptance. It is also consistent with the attempt being made in present youth movements. This change in interaction and the development of the self, if expressed in all institutions, would be reinforcing and might grow rather rapidly, in the process changing the institutions to allow further changes in the self.

Religion

The type of religious system that appears to be emerging from the youth culture is somewhat difficult to describe. Essentially, it is a humanistic religion that revolves around the statement, "Thou art God." Rather than postulating God as an authority who issues orders, this system stresses the unity of man, God, and nature. It borrows from Eastern religions, especially as interpreted by Watts (1966). In addition, there seems to be a tendency to follow the Unitarian practice of accepting ideas from several religious leaders instead of having a set dogma. Thus, Christ, Buddha, Mohammed, and other leaders are accepted as having something important to say but not necessarily as being the only interpreters of truth. This type of religion would appear to be consistent with the development of other institutions which are somewhat open and flexible rather than resting on hierarchical distributions of authority. It would appear to be less alienating, since it promotes the idea that man is God and therefore is creator of his own destiny to some extent. This approach is clearly not new to the world. The exact form this type of religion will take as it develops is not clear but the general outlines would appear to be consistent with a society which rests upon a humanistic value system. It should be noted that this type of religion is quite different from the "Jesus Freak" movement which is more like past religious movements.

Legitimizing Canopies

Through the process of interaction, human beings create social institutions that are then legitimized as they are passed from generation to generation. In preindustrial societies, the main legitimation was provided by the religious institution, which provided a "sacred canopy" over the existing institutions, which were then seen as having been created by God (Berger, 1969). After the Protestant Reformation and with the rise of industrial societies, a plurality of religions had to compete for members and no religion could define social reality as before. Other forms of legitimation arose to replace religion. Most of the legitimation of present existing institutions is provided by the social sciences. Thus, economics provides the rationale and the justification for the present economic system, which is legitimized through the mystique of science. Likewise, sociology provides legitimation of existing organizational forms by asserting that stratification is functional and bureaucracy is the inevitable and most efficient form of organization in modern societies. Psychology provides a view of the nature of man based on the Freudian idea of the dualistic nature of man: an angel riding on the back of a wild animal, and a constant struggle between the id and the ego for control. Added to this is the behaviorist view of man as a sort of machine moved by extrinsic rewards and punishments. These views of the social sciences provide "scientific" validity for existing institutions. Man is by nature competitive, divided between his human and animal nature, and moved by rewards and punishments. Thus, the existing institutions are consistent with the nature of man, and other institutional arrangements are idealistic conceptions that could never occur.

The social sciences are all at present in a turmoil, as new approaches are being developed and old orthodoxies challenged. The conception of scarcity on which economics rests is being challenged by theorists such as Galbraith (1968) and Theobald (1963). The positivist mold of sociology is being challenged by a more humanistic model stressed by a large number of theorists, among them Berger, Becker, and Matza. The tendency of academic sociology to reify existing institutions by treating them as social facts is also being challenged and this could undermine the legitimating function of conservative sociology. Psychology has seen the rise of a "third force" of humanistic psychology championed by Maslow, Rogers, and May. These more humanistic conceptions of social science are especially popular among the young.

The changing conception of the social sciences can provide a legitimation for new institutions as they develop from the old. As a new version of the nature of man appears, this will provide a rationale and justification of a change in education and a corresponding change in our conception of what motivates persons to engage in meaningful activity. The model of man as moved by extrinsic rewards will probably give way to a conception of human beings engaging in meaningful activity on the basis of their self needs in a model of self-actualization.

At this point, it may be useful to sum up the main thrust of the changes I see occurring in the major institutions mentioned above. At present, industrial capitalism is organized in a rational, bureaucratic manner in order to perform labor work, which is deemed necessary to deal with scarcity. Its driving force is indirect self-acceptance, which is sought through upward mobility in a competitive lifestyle. It is geared to economic production through activities organized as jobs performed for extrinsic rewards. This orientation is consistent with a stage of development in which human societies are developing the technological base that will allow them to deal with scarcity. Although this system has essentially solved the problem for which it was designed, the reification of institutions will keep this social reality around beyond the time of its ecological need.

From the abundance produced by industrial capitalism, there is slowly emerging a new social reality. Our present ecological situation allows the development of a society geared to the satisfaction of human needs (especially self needs). This system will stress activities performed for intrinsic reasons. Freed from scarcity assumptions and the need for productive efficiency, society will be able to develop more flexible institutions, designed to meet the needs of the persons within them rather than adjusting humans to the needs of production. This change will require a new value-system and a new conception of man. These are currently emerging, especially in the present youth culture.

I see this change process as one of slow evolution. Changes will occur gradually in each of the institutions mentioned (as, indeed, they are already occurring). From the description above, it is apparent that I see the general thrust of the change in each of these institutions to be in the direction of a more flexible, humanistic society. However, since the change will be slow and evolutionary, it might not appear that any real change is occurring at all. However, the combined impact of the gradual changes in each institution will have a profound effect on society in the long run. After a relatively slow change in each institution has its effect, the rate of change will accelerate as persons educated in a different manner, with more economic options open to them through the existence of a guaranteed income, guided by a humanistic religion, and able in general to achieve greater direct self-acceptance in the changing families that have appeared, will begin to change the institutions even more in the direction of the satisfaction of human needs.

The new institutions will fit together so that they will support each other. Persons who have learned how to learn and develop their self-potential in the free schools of the future will not be as lost in a society in which it is not necessary to hold a job as the graduates of today's schools would be in such a situation. The decreasing need for jobholding will in turn permit a more flexible education to occur. Eventually, as greater numbers of people are able to develop more of their human potential and achieve direct self-acceptance, they will be able to handle the type of freedom the new institutions will permit.

While the latter stages of this process will see the integration of institutions into a consistent pattern, I do not expect the transition period to be without turmoil and a great deal of problems. Persons who have been raised in a system in which they have learned to seek indirect self-acceptance and perform for extrinsic rewards, are going to have a very difficult time adapting to a system in which they are expected to engage in activities performed for their own sake. However, since such mechanisms as the guaranteed income do permit a choice, those who need extrinsic rewards will still be able to find them.

It will be noted that I have not predicted any basic change in the system of production other than the freeing of many persons from the necessity to work. The free market, to the extent that it exists now, will continue to exist for some time. The type of mixed welfare-state capitalism that characterizes American society will continue to exist at least until the transformation of the institutions mentioned is nearly completed. Only very late in the game will the profit-oriented system of capitalism be replaced by a system of humanistic socialism. It is difficult to predict at what point this will become necessary or possible but we can discuss what it involves.

Socialism can only exist under conditions of economic abundance. Only when the physical needs of man are satisfied, can a society exist whose purpose is the development of human potential. A socialistic society does not exist primarily for the production of consumer goods. The production of things beyond the level of necessity is not a goal of socialism. Socialism seeks to provide the conditions under which men can make living, rather than producing the means for living, their main business. Its long-range aim is the abolition of labor work and of money. It should be apparent that no such society presently exists, since socialism can only arise after industrial capitalism has solved the problem of producing sufficient goods to satisfy man's basic needs.

Socialism, then, is not merely a modified version of capitalism in which the workers are better paid or there is a more equal distribution of wealth. It is a society radically different from capitalism (Fromm, 1961). It is based on a different conception of man, a different set of values, and different institutional arrangements. Activity in such a society is performed for its own sake and is never the means to some other end.

It should be apparent why I feel that socialism can only come about in the very long run and only after the present society has gone through the process of evolution described earlier in this chapter. Since socialism can only exist when men have become self-aware and autonomous, it will develop only when self-awareness becomes widespread in the society. For this to happen, a cultural revolution in which the basic values and underlying assumptions of the society slowly change, while institutions are modified through the interaction of human beings in everyday life, is necessary.

Socialism cannot be imposed from above by a benevolent elite that takes over after a political revolution. It is not possible to force men to be free, and freedom in a very radical sense is what socialism is all about. Socialism can only evolve from below as the consciousness of human beings is changed through changing conditions under which they engage in activity and interact. The changes I describe above are intended to allow activity to be performed for its own sake as often as possible. It is only through the process of engaging in free activity (or leisure work) that the self-awareness that is a precondition for the emergence of socialism can arise.

This does not mean, however, that a "revolution of consciousness" will automatically occur and thereby change the society. I have tried to indicate that a good deal of political activity will be necessary to accomplish the goal of a human society. This will involve changes in power and people do not yield power without a struggle. Organized leadership will be needed. However, such leadership cannot attempt to force people to be free. It can only attempt to make it possible to be free and to make people aware of the underlying assumptions of the present society.

I have only sketched the general outlines of the institutional changes I think will occur as the human society develops. One cannot speculate very profitably on the details of these changes, since they could take various forms, and will be shaped and created through the interaction of the human beings who are creating them. Institutions exist only as they are created by human interaction and cannot be imposed on a group of people. The general form of the economic, educational, family, and religious institutions will probably be something like that described above, but the specifics can only be worked out by the persons who create these new institutional forms.

I have also avoided predicting the amount of time all this will take. This is because the pace of these events will depend upon the actions of human beings, and these are often difficult to predict.

It should be noted that the process of evolution that I predict, will itself provide greater freedom and a more humanistic society. When, in the very long run, socialism finally does emerge, men will have been living in a human society for some time. This is very important and cannot be stressed enough. There will be no miracles and no overnight changes. There will be a long process of change in consciousness, change in institutions, and political struggle before a humanistic socialism can be developed. Only through the interaction of human beings under slowly changing conditions can a new society be developed. The present youth movements are an indication that the slow process of evolution is now underway.

TEN

Assorted Nightmares:
Other Possible Futures

Although I think the general trend of changes in recent times and the ecological base that has been created favor the development of a human society, it is not absolutely certain that we will indeed take this path. There are other possibilities and other potential futures. In predicting the general shape of the future, writers often imply that the future they describe is inevitable. I doubt that anything is inevitable. We can only say that certain things are probable providing that other conditions do not change beyond a predicted range of possibilities. I think it will be helpful to briefly look at some of the alternative futures that are possible and assess the likelihood that one of them will take place rather than the development of a human society.

Someone Pushes the Button

Our present younger generation is the first in history to live their entire lives with the threat of total destruction hanging over them. This has affected the young to some degree since not only has the future been uncertain, but it has been uncertain whether there will even be a future. Since man now has the capacity to destroy the entire planet, the possibility that he will actually do so has always been present.

There is no real way to determine the likelihood that the bomb will actually be dropped. Although the possibility is always there, most of us have to continue to act as though it weren't. Otherwise, we would not be able to function at all. Consequently, we will have to proceed as though the bomb will not be dropped. After all, if it is dropped, attempts to predict the form of future societies are meaningless anyway. This may appear to be avoiding a problem, and perhaps it is. The point, however, is that an atomic catastrophe would render useless all predictions based on its not occurring, and I'm not interested, in this book, in trying to outline the shape of a postatomic society, assuming that there was one. Consequently, I will duck the issue and go on to the next possible nightmare.

Eco-Catastrophe

Assuming the bomb isn't dropped, there is another possible disaster that could occur. The ecological balance of the planet could be destroyed by the continued pollution of the air, pollution of the oceans, destruction of forest land, and other adverse affects on the environment of the expansion-minded industrial state. Thus it is possible that, if we keep going at our present rate very long, the planet will become uninhabitable. Or, barring that, we might destroy the capacity of the land to provide food in the quantity to which we are accustomed. That is, we could find ourselves returned to a state of scarcity in which we would be hard put to provide enough food for the population that exists.

If this should happen, then our predictions of a future based on abundance are meaningless, and the old scarcity-based assumptions once again would take hold. We would then find that all our technological progress has been for nothing, and we would have to make the best we could out of a lower ecological niche or possibly face the prospect of disappearing altogether.

The possibility of an ecological disaster is very real. This is especially so since the problem derives directly from the nature of an expansion-minded industrial state with its throwaway excess production, its alienation from nature, and its inability, in its present form, to stop expanding. A few patchwork attempts to clean up the air and water are not likely to prevent disaster. Neither is it likely that we can count upon new technology saving us from the effects of our old technology. As long as we continue our present path, ecological disaster is highly likely. In many ways, the crucial factor may be whether or not we can begin building a human society before we are destroyed by our own excess production. I don't know what the odds are that ecological disaster will strike before we alter our present society, but I wouldn't want to bet against the possibility that we will never make it. All that can be done here is to try to change the course we are on before it is too late. As with atomic disaster, if ecological disaster occurs, all predictions based on maintaining our present industrial base are meaningless. In the same way, the form that human society might take following such an event is not of concern here, although it is interesting to speculate about such things. As with the first disaster, if the second occurs, this book is irrelevant.

Repression Comes Down

The youth culture frightens many of the older generation, especially the so-called Middle Americans. Middle Americans are heard to lament, "Everything I have believed in and worked for is under attack." While some emphasize the violence that accompanies the political wing of the youth movement, it is probably the cultural manifestations of the movement that are most unsettling to older people. The youth culture flaunts those aspects of the self that the conventional straw-man image of the adjusted person attempts to hide. The erotic, expressive, fun-loving aspects of the human potential are trotted out and given free reign in open sight of people who have been taught to repress and deny these aspects of themselves. This can be very unsettling. In addition, to work hard for some goal most of your life and then be told that the goal is worthless, can lead to great dislike of the person or persons who tells one such a thing. To have invested most of your life in something and then to be confronted with a belief-system that invalidates your actions produces dissonance, and in such instances people will act to reaffirm their value-system. Certainly, studies of Middle Americans indicate that there is a great deal of potential hostility toward the dissident young. Further, a large majority of the American population supported the action of the police during the Chicago police riots in 1968 and the action of the National Guard during the Kent State shootings in 1970. This has led many young people to fear that the government would exploit these feelings in an attempt to bring about a crackdown on blacks and the radical young. Some even see a strong possibility of a totalitarian rightwing police-state emerging.

Certainly, the possibility of a totalitarian regime emerging in the United States can't be overlooked. The possibility is always there and increases in times of turmoil and change. Some of the actions of the present Administration hint at the possibility of some sort of repression or crackdown. There has been a quite different use made of the Justice Department by Attorney General Mitchell than by his predecessor Ramsey Clark (Harris, 1970). The passage of no-knock laws and the increased use of wiretaps, certainly pose a threat to civil liberties in this country. During the 1970 election campaigns, a rather overt attempt was made to play on the fears of Middle Americans for political advantage. Rather strident cries for law-and-order were heard throughout the land, and opponents of the Administration were called radic-libs or smeared with attempts to link them with revolutionaries. The assumption seemed to be that the silent majority would then rise up and support the Administration in its attempt to rid the country of "scum."

All of this is rather frightening. However, if we look at the results of the 1970 elections, there is no sign in those results that this strategy worked. The law-and-order issue was co-opted by the opposition and thereby neutralized. It does not seem to have much vote-getting potential in the near future. The dislike of the radical young still exists, but it doesn't seem as likely that it can be politically exploited.

The greatest danger to freedom probably comes not from the possibility of Middle America turning into a mass version of *Joe* and killing its young, but rather from governmental agencies such as the FBI and CIA. The controversy over FBI wiretapping of members of Congress in 1971 is a case in point.

There still exists a real danger in the assault on civil liberties. This should not be minimized, and we will have to remember that "eternal vigilance is the price of liberty." However, we need also to remember that attempts to destroy political freedom in the United States have been quite common in the past, running from the Alien and Sedition Acts to the McCarthy era. So far, we have managed to withstand any full-fledged trend toward a totalitarian society. This does not necessarily mean that we will be able to do so in the future, of course. Further turmoil, a collapse of the economy, or other unforeseen events could give further strength to an attempt to impose a police state. The political activity of the police also presents a danger. To be fair, we must keep in mind that the methods advocated by some radicals to promote their cause are as much of a threat to civil liberties as the efforts of the right wing. The main reason I haven't stressed these as much is that I don't think the authoritarian left has the power to impose their form of control, while the authoritarian right does have this power.

However, in order to impose a full-scale police state, it would probably be necessary to destroy the economy in the process. A system that runs on abundance and the ability to make profits by selling books, movies, and other media that deal with controversial ideas is not consistent with the imposition of a totalitarian regime. It would probably require a 1984 type of setup with no technological advance, enforced scarcity, and the like, in order to institute large-scale repression.

This, of course, does not mean that it won't happen. The danger is very real, especially if we are going through as large a transition as I have suggested. The future in this area is very uncertain. About all we can do is be very alert and hope for the best. The greatest danger may actually be a result of excessive fear on the part of liberals, who in their attempts to save the universities and prevent repression from the right, will repress anyone they see as shaking things up too much. This is especially likely in the universities where students and radical faculty might possibly be done in by liberals who are trying to save themselves by getting rid of the troublemakers. One has to be on guard against repression from conservatives, radicals, and even the supposedly pure liberals. At any rate, it will require alertness to avoid repression, but repression isn't inevitable if we keep our cool.

Superindustrialism

Assuming none of the disasters mentioned above occurs, there is another possible future that would prevent the development of a human society. Industrial societies could grow to be merely larger versions of what we have now.

Under this assumption, there would continue to be tremendous advances in science and technology. The biological sciences would experience an explosion in information and accomplishment. The environmental crisis would be solved by new technological advances. As the tertiary sector of the economy became automated, a quadrary level would arise, based on huge psych-corps that would provide people with "experiences" (Toffler, 1970). This would keep intact full employment, economic expansion, and other characteristics of the present society. While there would be many and varied surface changes, the basic values and thrust of the society would not be significantly altered.

The youth culture would become institutionalized in the superindustrial state as a phase through which people would go before assuming their adult roles. The youth movements would not lead to any significant changes in the society, but would be tolerated as a stage of life occupied by the idealistic young. They might even be provided with special reservations where they could smoke grass, fuck, and play around to their heart's content. Of course, the market would continue to exploit the youth culture and to expand the Pepsi generation.

The society would become more highly organized, more professionalized, more technocratic, with technologists assuming ever more important positions. Education would become more geared to producing people with scientific and technological expertise. Those who wanted humanistic education might be given special colleges where they could "do their thing" as long as they didn't bother those who were running the society.

This future, in many respects, seems like the most likely of any I have discussed. While it would involve technological and scientific changes, it would not involve any basic change in the organization of the society nor the values on which it is run. Conventional wisdom in sociology would support the notion that some version of superindustrialism is on its way. Since most of the assumptions of sociology about the nature of societies were developed during the earlier and present industrial eras, they assume that the structure of those periods, with perhaps modest changes, is inevitable in the future.

It should be noted that there is a rather fine line between the development of superindustrialism and the development of the human society. Since scientific and technological advances would continue in both, and since both would be based on the ecological base that already exists, it might be difficult, in the early stages, even to be sure which way the society was evolving. The main differences in the early stages would be subtle differences in institutions and differences in the way self-concepts are developed. In the long run, of course, there would be an enormous difference, as the small differences accumulate. It is difficult to be unbiased in predicting one or the other of these futures. There is a tendency to predict that one with which a person would feel most comfortable. Thus, radicals and youth-culture adherents tend toward predicting a human society, while corporate liberals and professional social scientists tend toward predicting the superindustrial state.

What is important is that an advanced technological society has a tremendous capacity to absorb dissident movements without significantly altering its basic form. If American Oil can give us daisies to put on our cars, anything is possible.

There are two factors that I see operating against the superindustrial society. One is the youth culture itself and the change in values that is occurring in it. To the extent that greater numbers of people engage in the great refusal to seek higher status and more consumer goods, superindustrialism would have problems./I am aware that there is a good possibility that youth-culture adherents will be absorbed into mainstream culture as they grow older/ The youth culture itself is a very marketable item, and young people trying to be hip can be sold a lot of artificial counter-culture crap. I am also aware that the youth culture adherents could be tolerated as a kind of exotic sideshow, as the ever-expanding industrial state rolls on. A lot depends on how fast the value-change spreads.

The other factor that makes ever-continuing growth and expansion unlikely is, of course, the environmental crisis. If I am right in my assumption that the heart of the problem is in the economic system itself, then we are either going to have to begin changing toward a human society or face ecological catastrophe. Here, as in so many other things, only time will tell.

I think the general trends that are occurring favor the development of a human society. However, I do not think this is inevitable, and any of the nightmares discussed above could occur instead. Much will depend on which version of reality and which ideological scheme eventually wins out as the future unfolds. It is difficult for the objective analyst to admit it, and most won't, but ultimately there is an ideological bend to their analyses, and this affects very much what we see as likely to happen. What I want to avoid here is the implication that a human society is inevitable and all we need do is sit back and wait for the grass to grow up through the concrete. If we do this, we are likely to be sitting on the last patch of grass just before they pave paradise and put up a parking lot. I don't look forward to paying a dollar and a half to see the trees.

ELEVEN

Conclusions

From an ecological perspective, ways of life are a product of conditions of life. Materials available in the environment flow through the ecosystem as energy is expended through work. The active agents in this process are human beings as they express themselves and attempt to make sense of the world through externalization. Through interaction with other humans, men create both material items (technology) and nonmaterial items (social reality). As these are created, both react on those who created them so that the environment, both physical and cultural, constantly changes.

The salient feature of human evolution on the planet Earth has been the expansion of man's niche in the ecosystem. This has been accomplished by 1) an increase in numbers (population), sustained by 2) increased resourcefulness in extracting needed supplies of energy and materials from the environment (technology), and 3) an elaboration of the patterns that organize human collective efforts involved in this activity (organization) (Duncan, 1964, p. 40). Over time, human society has moved in the direction of increasing complexity, higher ecological efficiency, and augmented variety.

The human animal appears to have two types of general needs: physical needs (need for food, water, oxygen, activity, sex, etc.) and self needs (need for an accurate and acceptable self-concept, need to expand the self-concept through interaction, and need to expand the self through action). Both of these types of needs can be satisfied in many different ways. That is, since the human animal is characterized by general needs, there is no set instinctual way of satisfying these needs. Humans can satisfy their need for food in various ways and the particular foods preferred in a society will be culturally determined.

Most of the activity of human beings on the planet Earth has been directed toward the economic problem of satisfying their physical needs. Men have engaged in economic activity to produce enough food, clothing, and other material items for man as an organism to survive. While the self needs are always important, they do not become a primary concern until there is sufficient economic abundance to ensure that the physical needs will be satisfied.

Until the Industrial Revolution, production of economic goods proceeded slowly. The breakdown of feudal society over a long period of time from the twelfth century, and the corresponding rise of capitalism and the "spirit" that went with it, set the stage for the enormous expansion of productivity that took place after 1800. This allowed, for the first time, the possibility of producing sufficient economic goods to meet the demand.

The capitalist form of activity came about as economic surplus allowed goods to be produced for purposes of exchange. Before exchange became an overriding aspect of human production, goods were produced mainly for use. As exchange spread, human activity became focused around the production of goods for exchange. Most production, then, was the production of commodities that could be exchanged in the market. Money became the universal standard of exchange: all commodities, including human labor, could be bought and sold for money. As all goods become commodities, so all human activity is transformed into jobs (labor work). Capitalist society then is characterized by the production of commodities through activities performed as jobs. Along with this is an increased division of labor, which increases efficiency through specialization. Human activity is then fragmented, and this fragmented activity is performed for extrinsic rewards.

Along with the change in the form of economic activities that occurred with the development of industrial capitalism, there was also a change in the form of human association from that of *Gemeinschaft* to that of *Gesellschaft* (Tönnies, 1957). A *Gemeinschaft* is a social unit to which one belongs more or less automatically, such as a family. The members of a *Gemeinschaft* are bound to each other as whole persons. *Gesellschaft* involves a contractual form of association in which humans associate through conscious design for some specific purpose. Individuals associate in a *Gesellschaft* with only part of their being, that part which is related to the purpose of the organization. When interacting in the *Gesellschaft* form of association, humans learn to play the social roles appropriate for the specific purpose of that association, and to leave out—and indeed hide—those aspects of the self inappropriate for that association. This is efficient and allows humans to interact for specific purposes with other humans whom they do not know. The most common form of association under industrial capitalism is *Gesellschaft*. Thus as goods become interchangeable through being transformed into commodities and activity becomes interchangeable through being transformed into jobs, so human beings become interchangeable through being transformed into social roles. Thus human production, human activity, and parts of the self all become commodities that can be exchanged through the medium of money. This allows an efficiency in production that enables humans to produce goods beyond the wildest dreams of preindustrial societies.

Of course, there is also a disadvantage to this process. Since most of human association is on the basis of fragments of the self, there are few chances to relate to other human beings as whole persons. This makes it difficult, if not impossible, to form an accurate and acceptable self-concept, since humans in industrial societies are rarely exposing all of what they are to other human beings. This is especially so since there is a tendency to reify the social roles we play and to create a social straw man, which consists of the public selves of human beings and which implies that those aspects of the self that do not fit with this straw man are unacceptable and that persons who have these unacceptable aspects of self are therefore unacceptable. This is the process I have referred to as the universal fake-out.

Industrial capitalism is characterized by the production of commodities through activities performed as jobs, which are specialized through intense division of labor and association, which is characterized by *Gesellschaft*. It involves an impersonal form of life in which relations with other human beings involve a calculation of what can be gained through the association and in which human beings are in constant competition with each other for rewards assumed to be scarce. The attempt to gain indirect self-acceptance through accumulation of these rewards ensures that these rewards will continue to appear scarce, since it is impossible ever to gain self-acceptance indirectly.

The culture of industrial capitalism emphasizes the production of commodities and the accumulation of wealth. Consequently, it emphasizes as acceptable those aspects of the self that are congruent with this end. Thus it is the rational, instrumental, competitive, acquisitive portions of the human whole that are emphasized in the social straw man. Further, these aspects of the self are seen to be the appropriate aspects of that portion of the population that is most involved in the main source of identity in industrial societies: occupation. Those who are most involved in the labor market are those who are expected to have the acceptable aspects of self and who are consequently those who have the highest status in the society. On the basis of age, race, and sex, the group that is most involved in occupation and has the highest status is that of middle-aged white men. They are expected to be the carriers of the instrumental aspects of self that are so valued in modern societies. However, the other aspects of self do not disappear. As we saw earlier, they still exist but cannot be expressed by those who are not supposed to have them. Consequently, they are projected onto those groups in the society that are, to some extent, kept out of the labor market; and those groups, as well as those aspects of self, have a lower status. On the basis of age, race, and sex, we can identify three such groups and the aspects of self associated with them.

The young are expected to be idealistic, playful, and hedonistic. These low-status aspects of self are felt to be fine for those low-status persons who are allowed to express them, but inappropriate for those who are producing (that is, holding jobs). Blacks are expected to be erotic, lazy, and hedonistic. These qualities, of course, do not suit them well for jobs, so they, like the young, are to a large extent excluded from occupations, especially high-status occupations. Women are expected to be expressive and emotional; thus women, like those aspects of the self associated with them, have a low status. The idealistic, erotic, and expressive aspects of self are subordinated to the instrumental aspects of self, and the groups expected to carry those subordinate aspects of self are subordinate to the group that carries the instrumental aspects. After all, it is fine to be idealistic, erotic, or expressive, but those who are these things are not taken seriously. And, of course, persons in each of the categories associated with certain aspects of the self are not expected to display the inappropriate characteristics. Woe to the instrumental woman or expressive man.

I don't think it is a coincidence that we are at present seeing a drive for equality by blacks, women, and the young simultaneously. I think that this simultaneous drive suggests that the culture of industrial capitalism is disintegrating and the low status or inappropriate aspects of self are beginning to become acceptable. This implies that the culture and its straw-man image are changing. I think this is a process that has been going on for some time as the ecological conditions that produced industrial capitalism have changed.

The increased ability to satisfy the physical needs through the increased production made possible by the Industrial Revolution, might be expected to lead to an increased concern with the self needs and to a form of social organization intended to allow satisfaction of those needs. This didn't happen because production of commodities and consumption became ends in themselves, as did work.

The emphasis on work that characterized the Protestant Ethic, led to work becoming an end in itself. Since the social institutions that emerged with industrial capitalism provided no other way for a person to have the right to consume, labor became necessary whether or not it was needed for production. In addition, the culture of capitalism did not provide any meaningful preparation for the use of leisure. The basic value-system of the society emphasized the need for full employment with make-work programs, featherbedding, and other means of creating jobs. Further, since the ideology of American society holds that men should not be allowed to consume if they do not produce, and there is an intense fear that people will not want to work if they are given subsistence without work, it has not been possible to provide basic food, shelter, and clothing as a matter of right (Macarov, 1970).

The Protestant Ethic and the culture of industrial capitalism stressed production, hard work, and the accumulation of wealth as the primary goals in life. Most of the American way of life came to be oriented toward achieving those goals. However, there was at the same time an undercurrent of rejection of these goals and an attempt to emphasize a more humanistic way of life. The alternative set of values has been advocated mainly by intellectuals, beatniks, and other groups somewhat removed from the workaday world.

There have been in the United States and Europe a number

of movements emphasizing the ideological themes which are seen today in the counter-culture. In the early nineteenth century in Europe, this was expressed in many diverse forms, ranging from socialism to withdrawal into bohemian communities. With the development of bohemian communities, such as Greenwich Village, during the first decade of this century, the attempt to establish an alternative value-system was also present in the United States. ". . . American intellectuals expressed their disaffection in a variety of ways: muckraking journalism, little magazine literary and social criticism, realistic novels, avantgarde poetry and painting, solon conversation, scholarly radicalism, progressive politics, labor organizing, the socialist movement" (Flacks, 1971, p. 227). The intellectual radicalism that developed emphasized that cultural renaissance, political reconstruction, and character transformation were all part of the same process and were all necessary to change the existing society.

The criticism of the culture of industrial capitalism by European and American intellectuals was incorporated into the value-systems of many middle-class Americans, especially those who had attended college. "So the making of the American intelligentsia depended first on the rise in society of occupations devoted to education, socialization, social control, the creation and distribution of culture, and the rise of a large mass of people to enter these occupations; and, second, it depended on the existence of tiny groups of avant-garde intellectuals who began to work out values and ideological perspectives suitable for these occupations and the persons who held them" (Flacks, 1971, p. 229).

The value-system that emerged from the intellectual critique of industrial capitalism was implemented in the educational system and also in the childraising patterns of at least a subgroup of the middle class. This means that the children of this subgroup were raised with a value-system somewhat at odds with the mainstream value-system. The middle-class family tended to be less authoritarian, less hierarchical, more child-centered and more democratic than the working class family or the traditional American family. The experience of being raised in these families provided a predisposition toward a humanistic value system and some discomfort upon encountering other institutions.

Slater (1970) suggests that there are three desires that are provided for in the middle-class American family but that are deeply frustrated by American culture as a whole. These are the desire for community, the desire for engagement, and the desire for independence. The disjunction between the emphasis on these values in the middle-class family and the emphasis on their opposites in mainstream society, can be seen as one source of discontent among middle-class youth when they encounter institutions such as the university.

The humanistic value-system that was stressed in the families of a subgroup of the middle class and that was reinforced in the critical environment of the university, began to reach an increased proportion of the population as increased affluence led to the expansion of education. There came to be located on American college campuses in the late fifties and the sixties large numbers of people who had been kept out of the labor market for such a long period of their lives that they had not grown used to the workaday world of industrial capitalism. This was a population that took affluence for granted and had a predisposition to humanistic values. At the same time, the increased pluralism of complex industrial society had rendered transparent the social reality of mainstream society (Kelly, 1972). The alternative realities available in a pluralistic society, and the exposure to alternate cultures through education, tend to make persons aware of the nature of their society's social reality. That is, if discrepant social worlds are available, there will be an increasing general consciousness of the relativity of all social worlds. Combined with the change in the ecological base that came about as industrialism matured, this awareness of the relativity of all social reality led to an intense questioning of the underlying assumptions of the culture of mainstream society. This was aided by events such as poverty in the midst of plenty, the discontent of racial minorities, and the Vietnam War, none of which could be adequately explained by the legitimizing machineries of the prevailing reality.

The counter-culture movement of the sixties, then, is another step in a long process of slow undermining of the Protestant Ethic and the culture of capitalism. It took past criticisms of that culture and carried them a bit further, and of course the population involved in this criticism was larger than ever before due to the expansion of affluence and education. In terms of the "ethic" which guides a culture, there had been a slow erosion of the Protestant Ethic for some time.

Especially after World War II, the Protestant Ethic in its extreme form has been undermined by increased affluence and changing morality. The existence of the welfare state contradicted much of the rhetoric associated with the Puritan worldview. There became an increasing emphasis on consumption, on pleasure, on buying on credit instead of saving for a rainy day. Middle-class America as a whole had moved to a form of Social Ethic.

From the Protestant Ethic stressing somber virtues, hard work, pragmatism, and moderation, society moved to the Social Ethic of work and play, family and politics, and the good life in the suburbs. Today's youth, with their increased awareness of the self needs, moved beyond the Social Ethic to the Hang Loose Ethic.

The Hang Loose Ethic emphasizes irreverence (a rejection of the absolute truth of the sanctity of marriage, chastity, civil obedience, respect for authority, and "My country right or wrong"), humanism (stressing the value of human beings and the full development of human life), spontaneity (the ability to groove with what's currently happening), tolerance (emphasizing the right of individuals to do what they want as long as they don't step on others), and the pursuit of experience (the importance of trying different things now).

Ironically, the values expressed in this ethic are derived from some of the highest ideals of western man. These are essentially the ideals that are given lip service throughout American society but that are compromised in the process of "growing up" and "being realistic." They are the values that have existed as a secondary value system in American society and as the primary value system of disaffected intellectuals and bohemians. It should not be surprising that a group of young people, freed from the need to accept adult roles until they are nearly thirty, would begin to take seriously the ideals that have been drummed into them by their culture while rejecting the practices of that culture, which contradict the ideals.

Flacks (1970) tends to see the intelligentsia and their children as a new social class with revolutionary potential. I doubt if the intellectuals can truly be seen as a class in this sense. For one thing, a very large portion of this group is basically conservative in its orientation. That is, anything that threatens their jobs and their comfortable standard of living will be opposed. Since most attempts radically to transform society do threaten the lifestyles and worldview of professionals, much of this group strongly opposes any such changes. "A liberal is a person who is ten degrees to the left in good times and ten degrees to the right when it gets close to home." I have seen too many professional academics panic at the mere thought of having students serve with them on committees, to expect much revolutionary action from this group.

It is difficult to be truly revolutionary when you are the members of a favored class. Those who are well off simply have too much to lose. The young, who haven't yet invested much in the existing order, can be more radical than those who have a lot to lose. However, I would agree that at least some of the intelligentsia are radical or revolutionary. I just don't see a revolutionary class here.

Conclusions

On the other hand, I think Flacks is right when he says that "capitalism cannot readily absorb the cultural aspirations that have emerged in this group—aspirations toward the abolition of alienated labor and the achievement of democratic community" (Flacks, 1971, p. 238). I also agree that it is unlikely that the culture of capitalism can survive the affluence which it produces.

Human beings expand their niche in the ecosystem by producing technology, which, when coupled with new forms of social organization, brings about an enormous potential to produce consumer goods. The rise of capitalism and the consequent Industrial Revolution brought about an increase in the ability of men to produce goods that went far beyond anything which had occurred before. For this system to function efficiently, however, intense division of labor was necessary with consequent *Gesellschaft* form of association, alienated activity, alienated aspects of self, and a social order geared almost totally to the production and accumulation of economic goods.

This very economic wealth, in turn, allowed an increasing number of people in the society to be freed from primary, secondary, and even tertiary activities within the economic system, and to engage in activities directly connected with neither resource extraction nor the production and distribution of consumer goods. However, the existing cultural system and the one-factor distribution system that goes with it do not provide any way to perform quadrary activities other than transforming them into jobs with the same orientation as the rest of society. However, the increasing affluence and extent of education in American society allows more and more emphasis to be placed upon the humanistic value-system that has always existed in a secondary way in American culture. When large numbers of persons attempt to practice this value-system as a primary one, they come into conflict with the prevailing culture. Thus, as Schumpeter (1950) expected, the intellectual attacks have begun to destroy the culture of industrial capitalism.

But, is this likely to lead to a revolution in advanced industrial societies? A lot, of course, depends on what we mean by revolution. In its strict sense, revolution is "an attempt—sometimes successful, sometimes unsuccessful—to seize power on the part of political forces avowedly opposed not merely to the existing regime but to the existing social order as a whole" (Lasch, 1971, p. 919). Thus, a coup d'état, which merely changes the group in power, or a rebellion, which usually attacks symbols of oppression, are not revolutions. A revolution, which is not necessarily violent, aims at bringing about a new social order.

We have seen that the actions of most out-groups in American society have been rebellions, attempts to drive central authority out of the group's territory. We have, in elections, mini-coups on a regular basis, and these keep the population from growing to hate political leaders. A revolution is another matter.

I have suggested that a revolution can only occur over several generations since there is needed a long period of softening and disintegration of the existing social reality before the final step of an actual change in political power is possible. I think that the process of disintegration of the culture of capitalism has been proceeding for some time, but that American society is still a generation or two away from the point where there will have been a sufficient cultural change to allow a shift in the ownership of the means of production, an end to production for profit, and the advent of humanistic socialism. I have also suggested that this is not inevitable, since there are other possible futures which could occur.

We must keep in mind, when considering the possibility of revolution in America, that revolutionary models based on European revolutions and Third World revolutions probably do not apply. These revolutions occurred in predominantly rural societies undergoing rapid change. They were directed against authoritarian states that essentially nourished a revolutionary negation of themselves by relying more and more on naked force, which made counter-force the only possible response.

Advanced industrial societies are much more flexible, and rule through an elaborate network of civil institutions, and will encourage dissident movements to struggle for control of these institutions, thus, making the dissent reformist rather than revolutionary. Further, as Lasch (1971, p. 324) notes, "Industrial society has not eliminated poverty but it has eliminated the hungry mob as a force in history."

Modern youth movements, then, will not lead to a revolution, or will they by themselves bring about any meaningful social change. Youth, as a group, are economically superfluous, and are consequently unlikely to affect significantly the system of production and distribution of economic goods. The mass swarmings of the young, such as the April 1971 March on Washington, are interesting in that they show that there are large numbers of dissatisfied persons who can be mobilized for some causes. However, despite the serious intent of many of the young during these swarmings, they do, after all, represent an occasion to have a certain amount of fun and the type of luxury in which a leisure class can afford to engage. A transformation of American society will require a coalition of many groups, as I suggested earlier. This may be difficult to bring about, but it seems to be essential.

Thus, the story of the student movement in the United States over the past decade is a story of continued self-transformation. Once student activism was characteristic of tiny groups of campus rebels —the offspring (as we have suggested) of the educated middle class who, facing severe value and vocational crises and finding no moral way to assimilate into American society, searched for a new basis for living in cultural avant-gardism and moralistic dedication to social reform. In the past decade, the movement has obviously spread well beyond this original group. It has transformed itself from a nonideological movement for vague principles of social vision and a new framework for social criticism, finally into a movement spearheaded by revolutionaries tending to look more and more to classical revolutionary doctrine for guiding principles for their own action. It is a movement that both rejects and is frustrated by its roots in the intelligentsia. It has expressed and articulated most clearly the fundamental aspirations of that class for a new social order in which men can achieve autonomy in determining the conditions of their lives, in which hierarchy and domination are replaced by community and love, in which war, militarism, and imperialism are obsolete, and in which class and racial distinctions are abolished. It is a movement that has provided an opportunity for thousands of young people to express their aspirations directly in terms of the ongoing political struggle and (perhaps more crucially) in terms of a way of life and set of vocations that the larger society denies. It is, then, a movement of surprising strength. It has touched the minds of millions and changed the lives of thousands of young people. It has severely shaken the stability of the American Empire and has challenged the basic assumptions of its culture. But its most sensitive adherents have increasingly despaired as the movement has reached the limit of its possibilities. As we have seen, this despair is rooted first in the unresponsiveness of the political system to pressure for reform; second, in the narrow class base of the movement; and third, in the seemingly overwhelming capacity of the authorities to manage social control. Despair generates the urgency of revolution as necessity; the movement must transcend its social base; it must make common cause with other enemies of the empire around the world. [Flacks, 1971, pp. 251–252]

If the alternative culture is to have any chance of bringing about real change, then it must expand beyond the limits of a youth movement. This means that it will have to become more than a movement for a favored leisure class. Further, it will have to appeal to other groups in terms acceptable and meaningful to those groups. The environmental crisis provides one way of doing this. The environmental issue can be used as a distraction to keep people from being concerned about civil rights and the war, or it can be used to focus attention on those aspects of industrial capitalism that are harmful. That is, if the environmental crisis is seen as merely a matter of picking up litter and using returnable bottles, it can be easily co-opted, and we will merely get more commercials from the corporations telling us how much they are doing to provide clean air. On the other hand, if it can be shown that the environmental crisis has its roots in a system that produces for profit, and indeed produces for the sake of producing, then a wider range of the population may begin to ask questions about exactly what is going on.

At any rate, it is essential that the present dissident movements not allow themselves to be defined strictly as a youth phenomenon. While there are important generational aspects in what is now happening, I have tried to show throughout this book that there is more to the process than that. However, it is very convenient for the government, with the help of social scientists who explain the present unrest in terms of youthful rebellions against authority, to neutralize the movement by defining it as a problem of communication between generations. This draws attention away from asking fundamental questions about the social order in which we live.

First, any student and youth movement can become a relatively insulated expression of generational revolt. This is not the explicit intention of the New Left, but it appears to be the implicit expectation of many of the agencies of social control impinging upon the student movement. A generational movement may be understood as a movement of cultural and social innovation whose impact has been contained within the framework of existing society. For agencies of social control, the ideal circumstance would be the opportunity to eliminate the most disruptive and destructive elements in the movement, while effecting some of the cultural, social, and political innovations and reforms that the movement advocates. Thus, you put yippies in jail while working some means to legalize marijuana. You put draft resisters in jail or into exile while abolishing conscription. You expel SDS from the campus while admitting student representatives to the Board of Trustees. You deride and derogate the women's liberation movement while liberalizing abortion laws. You break up and harass hippie urban communities while providing fame and fortune to some rock music groups. This is all done with the aid of ideological perspectives which emphasize that what is going on is a generational revolt, that there is a generation gap, that the big problem is one of communication between the old and the young. The hope is that if reforms can be made to liberalize the cultural and social atmosphere (particularly in relation to sex, drug use, art, music, censorship, and so forth), the mass of youth will not be tempted by the message of the radical vanguard.

If the New Left were to be channeled more fully in the direction of generational revolt, it would then serve stabilizing and modernizing functions for the going system. It would not be the first time that a radical movement in the United States ended up this way, but from the viewpoint of New Left activists, such an outcome for the movement would represent profound failure, particularly if it meant (as it now seems to mean) that the most active and militant of the participants of the movement would suffer rather than benefit from any social change that might be forthcoming. There is a substantial likelihood that the main consequences of the student movement and the New Left of the 60s will be in this direction. The most important fact supporting this outcome is that the movement has, in the ten years of its existence, failed to break out of its isolation; it remains a movement of the young, particularly the relatively advantaged young. [Flacks, 1971, pp. 252–253]

The youth movements are important, however, in that they suggest that the affluence of industrial capitalism has produced groups that are developing an alternative social reality that will compete with mainstream reality, and by its very existence in the same society, tend to render the social reality of industrial capitalism transparent. "The revolutionary tradition effectively conceals the fact that in most modern revolutions, the overthrow of the old regime took place only after alternative patterns of culture had established themselves side by side with the dominant ones" (Lasch, 1971, p. 333). An alternative culture has been establishing itself alongside the culture of capitalism in American society for some time now. The present youthful unrest suggests that that alternative reality is growing stronger. It is hard to determine how long these competing social realities can exist side by side before the clash in their underlying assumptions leads to an awareness and questioning of the underlying assumptions of the culture of industrial capitalism. At that point, anything is possible. It is the task of those who are oriented toward the creation of a human society to see to it that the foundations are prepared, so that when the opportunity presents itself, we can move toward the realization of that vision.

BIBLIOGRAPHY

ONE / *On the Culture of Industrial Capitalism*

Becker, Howard S. 1966. "Whose Side Are We On?" *Social Problems* 14 (Winter):239–247.

Bennis, Warren G., and Slater, Philip. 1963. *The Temporary Society*. New York: Harper and Row.

Berger, Peter L. 1969. *The Sacred Canopy*. Garden City, N.Y.: Doubleday Anchor.

Berger, Peter L., and Luckmann, Thomas. 1966. *The Social Construction of Reality*. Garden City, N.Y.: Doubleday.

Berger, Thomas. 1970. *Vital Parts*. New York: Signet Books.

Brown, James Cooke. 1970. *The Troika Incident*. Garden City, N.Y.: Doubleday.

Davis, Kingsley, and Moore, Wilbert E. 1945. "Some Principles of Stratification." *American Sociological Review* 10 (April):242–249.

Davis, Wayne H. 1970. "Overpopulated America." *The New Republic* 162 (10 January):13–15.

Duncan, Otis Dudley. 1964. "Social Organization and The Ecosystem" (pp. 37–82). In Robert E. L. Faris, ed., *Handbook of Modern Sociology*. Chicago: Rand McNally.

Etzioni, Amitai. 1968. "Basic Human Needs, Alienation, and Inauthenticity." *American Sociological Review* 33 (December):870–885.

Fair, Charles M. 1970. *The Dying Self*. Garden City, N.Y.: Doubleday Anchor.

Faunce, William A. 1968. *Problems of An Industrial Society*. New York: McGraw-Hill.

Friedman, Milton. 1962. *Capitalism and Freedom*. Chicago: University of Chicago Press.

Fromm, Erich. 1955. *The Sane Society*. New York: Fawcett Premier Books.

Fromm, Erich. 1961. *Marx's Concept of Man*. New York: Frederick Ungar Publishing Co.

Fromm, Erich. 1963. *Beyond The Chains of Illusion*. New York: Pocket Books.

Bibliography

Galbraith, John Kenneth. 1968. *The New Industrial State*. New York: Signet Books.

Goffman, Erving. 1959. *The Presentation of Self in Everyday Life*. Garden City, N.Y.: Doubleday Anchor.

Green, Christopher. 1968. "Guaranteed Income Plans—Which One is Best?" *Trans-Action* 6 (January–February): 49–53.

Harris, Richard. 1970. *Justice*. New York: Avon Books.

Hawley, Amos H. 1950. *Human Ecology*. New York: The Ronald Press.

Jourard, Sidney M. 1964. *The Transparent Self*. Princeton, N. J.: Van Nostrand.

Karp, Herbert H., and Kelly, K. Dennis. 1971a. *Toward an Ecological Explanation of Inter-Metropolitan Migration*. Chicago: Markham Publishing Co.

Kelly, K. Dennis. 1972. "Rapid Change and Structural Disruption." In Peter K. Manning, ed., *Deviance and Change*. Englewood Cliffs, N.J.: Prentice-Hall.

Kelly, K. Dennis, and Chambliss, William J. 1966. "Status Consistency and Political Attitudes." *American Sociological Review* 31 (June): 375–382.

Kelso, Louis O., and Adler, Mortimer J. 1958. *The Capitalist Manifesto*. New York: Random House.

Kelso, Louis O., and Hetter, Patricia. 1969. *Two Factor Theory: The Economics of Reality*. New York: Vintage Books.

Keyserling, Leon. 1967. "Guaranteed Annual Incomes." *The New Republic* 156 (18 March): 20–23.

Laing, R. D. 1967. *The Politics of Experience*. New York: Ballantine Books.

Macarov, David. 1970. *Incentives to Work*. San Francisco: Jossey-Bass.

Mandel, Ernest. 1970. *Marxist Economic Theory*. 2 volumes. New York: Modern Reader Paperbacks.

Maslow, Abraham H. 1968. *Toward a Psychology of Being,* 2nd edition. Princeton, N. J.: Van Nostrand.

Mead, George Herbert. 1934. *Mind, Self and Society*. Chicago: University of Chicago Press.

Montagu, Ashley. 1967. *The Human Revolution*. New York: Bantam Books.

Pappenheim, Fritz. 1968. *The Alienation of Modern Man*. New York: Modern Reader Paperbacks.

Putney, Snell, and Putney, Gail. 1964. *The Adjusted American*. New York: Harper and Row.

Schaar, John H. 1970. "Reflections on Authority." *New American Review* 1 (January): 44–81.

Schumpeter, Joseph. 1950. *Capitalism, Socialism and Democracy*. New York: Harper and Bros.

Stanley, Manfred. 1968. "Nature, Culture, and Scarcity: Foreword to a

Theoretical Synthesis." *American Sociological Review* 33 (December):855–870.

Theobald, Robert. 1963. *Free Men and Free Markets*. Garden City, N.Y.: Doubleday Anchor.

Theobald, Robert, ed. 1965. *The Guaranteed Income*. Garden City, N.Y.: Doubleday Anchor.

Theobald, Robert, ed. 1969. *Committed Spending*. Garden City, N.Y.: Doubleday Anchor.

Tobin, James. 1967. "It Can Be Done! Conquering Poverty in the U.S. by 1976." *The New Republic* 156 (3 June):14–18.

Toffler, Alvin. 1970. *Future Shock*. New York: Random House.

Tönnies, Ferdinand. 1957. Community and Society [*Gemeinschaft und Gesellschaft*]. Translated by C. P. Loomis. East Lansing: Michigan State University.

Watts, Alan W. 1963. *Psychotherapy East and West*. New York: Mentor Books.

Weber, Max. 1958. *The Protestant Ethic and The Spirit of Capitalism*. New York: Charles Scribner's Sons.

White, Theodore H. 1969. *The Making of the President 1968*. New York: Atheneum.

Young, Wayland. 1966. *Eros Denied: Sex in Western Society*. New York: Grove Press.

TWO / *On Youth and Youth Culture*

Aldridge, John W. 1970. *In the Country of the Young*. New York: Harper and Row.

Ambrosino, Lillian. 1971. *Runaways*. Boston: Beacon Press.

Berger, Bennett M. 1971. *Looking For America: Essays on Youth, Suburbia, and Other American Obsessions*. Englewood Cliffs, N. J.: Prentice-Hall.

Berger, Peter L., and Berger, Brigitte. 1971. "The Blueing of America." *The New Republic* 164 (3 April):20–23.

Bottomore, T. B. 1969. *Critics of Society*. New York: Vintage Books.

Braden, William. 1970. *The Age of Aquarius*. Chicago: Quadrangle Books.

Brown, Michael E. 1969. "The Condemnation and Persecution of Hippies." *Trans-Action* 6 (September):33–46.

Capouya, Emile. 1971. "The Myth of Ecstatic Community." *The Nation* (18 January):85–87.

Cleaver, Eldridge. 1968. *Soul On Ice*. New York: Delta Books.

Cohen, Albert. 1967. "Middle-Class Delinquency and The Social Structure" (pp. 203–207). In Edmund W. Vaz, ed., *Middle-Class Juvenile Delinquency*. New York: Harper and Row.

Cowan, Paul. 1970. *The Making of An Un-American*. New York: Delta Books.

Bibliography

Davis, Fred. 1967. "Why All of Us May Be Hippies Someday." *Trans-Action* 5 (December):10–18.

Douglas, Jack D. 1970. *Youth in Turmoil*. Washington: U.S. Government Printing Office.

Eisenstadt, S. N. 1956. *From Generation to Generation*. New York: The Free Press.

Farber, Jerry. 1969. *The Student As Nigger*. Los Angeles: Contact Books.

Feuer, Lewis. 1969. *The Conflict of Generations*. New York: Basic Books.

Flacks, Richard. 1970. "Social and Cultural Meanings of Student Revolt: Some Informal Comparative Observations." *Social Problems* 17 (Winter):340–358.

Flacks, Richard. 1971. "Revolt of the Young Intelligentsia: Revolutionary Class-Consciousness in a Post-Scarcity America" (pp. 223–263). In Roderick Aya and Norman Miller, eds., *The New American Revolution*. New York: The Free Press.

Friedenberg, Edgar Z. 1964. *The Vanishing Adolescent*. New York: Delta Books.

Friedenberg, Edgar Z. 1966. "Adolescence as a Social Problem" (pp. 35–75). In Howard S. Becker, ed., *Social Problems: A Modern Approach*. New York: John Wiley and Sons.

Garbo, Norman. 1970. *The Movement*. New York: Pyramid Books.

Goodman, Paul. 1960. *Growing Up Absurd*. New York: Vintage Books.

Gottlieb, David, and Ramsey, Charles E. 1964. *The American Adolescent*. Homewood, Illinois: Dorsey Press.

Holt, John. 1964. *How Children Fail*. New York: Delta Books.

Karp, Herbert H., and Kelly, K. Dennis. 1971b. "Toward an Explanation of The Emergence of Contemporary Youth Culture." Unpublished manuscript. East Lansing: Michigan State University.

Keniston, Kenneth. 1968. *Young Radicals*. New York: Harcourt, Brace and World.

Killian, Lewis M. 1964. "Social Movements" (pp. 426–455). In Robert E. L. Faris, ed. *Handbook of Modern Sociology*. Chicago: Rand McNally.

Knott, Paul D. 1971. *Student Activism*. Dubuque, Iowa: William C. Brown.

Kohák, Erazim. 1971. "Being Young in Postindustrial Society." *Dissent* 28 (February):30–40.

Krause, Charles A. 1971. "What's Left of the New Left." *The New Republic* 164 (20 March):17–18.

Lasch, Christopher. 1971. "Epilogue" (pp. 318–334). In Roderick Aya and Norman Miller, eds., *The New American Revolution*. New York: The Free Press.

Leonard, George B. 1968. *Education and Ecstasy*. New York: Delacorte Press.

Lipset, Seymour M. 1971. "Youth and Politics" (pp. 743–792). In Robert K. Merton and Robert Nisbet. eds., *Contemporary Social Problems*. New York: Harcourt Brace Jovanovich.

Lofland, John. 1968. "The Youth Ghetto." *Journal of Higher Education* 39 (March):121–143.

Mannheim, Karl. 1952. "The Problem of Generations" (pp. 276–322). In *Essays on The Sociology of Knowledge*. New York: Oxford University Press.

McCann, Charles J. 1970. "Introductory Remarks for Planning, Phase II." Olympia, Washington: Evergreen State College.

Newfield, Jack. 1967. *A Prophetic Minority*. New York: Signet Books.

Nisbet, Robert A., Starr, Roger, and Bromwich, David L. 1970. "The Counter-Culture and its Apologists." *Commentary* 50 (December): 40–59.

Postman, Neil, and Weingartner, Charles. 1969. *Teaching as a Subversive Activity*. New York: Delacorte Press.

Rapson, Richard L., ed. *The Cult of Youth in Middle Class America*. Lexington, Mass.: D. C. Heath and Co.

Reich, Charles A. 1970. *The Greening of America*. New York: Random House.

Rimmer, Robert H. 1967. *The Harrad Experiment*. New York: Bantam Books.

Robertson, Don, and Steele, Marion. 1971. *The Halls of Yearning*. San Francisco: Canfield Press.

Roszak, Theodore. 1969. *The Making of a Counter Culture*. Garden City, N.Y.: Doubleday Anchor.

Rubenstein, Richard E. 1970. *Rebels in Eden*. Boston: Little, Brown and Co.

Rubin, Jerry. 1970. *Do It!* New York: Simon and Schuster.

Scott, Marvin B., and Lyman, Stanford M. 1970. *The Revolt of the Students*. Columbus, Ohio: Charles E. Merrill.

Seale, Bobby. 1970. *Seize The Time*. New York: Vintage Books.

Silberman, Charles. 1970. *Crisis in the Classroom*. New York: Random House.

Simon, Geoffrey, and Trout, Grafton. 1967. "Hippies in College—from Teeny-Boppers to Drug Freaks." *Trans-Action* 5 (December):27–32.

Slater, Philip. 1970. *The Pursuit of Loneliness*. Boston: Beacon Press.

Walter, Robert H. K. 1964. *Stacy Tower*. New York: Bantam Books.

Watts, Alan W. 1966. *The Book*. New York: Collier Books.

Wolfe, Tom. 1969. *The Electric Kool-Aid Acid Test*. New York: Bantam Books.

Wolfe, Tom. 1969. *The Pump House Gang*. New York: Bantam Books.

Yankelovich, Daniel. 1969. *Generations Apart: A Study of the Generation Gap Conducted for CBS News*. New York: Columbia Broadcasting System.

ACKNOWLEDGMENTS

From *The Adjusted American* by Snell Putney and Gail J. Putney. Reprinted by permission of Harper & Row Publishers, Inc.

Taken from *Free Men and Free Markets* by Robert Theobald. © 1963 by Robert Theobald. Used by permission of Clarkson N. Potter, Inc.

From *The Greening of America* © 1970 by Charles A. Reich. Reprinted by permission of Random House, Inc.

Marx's Concept of Man by Erich Fromm. Reprinted by permission of the Frederick Ungar Publishing Co., Inc.

Reprinted with permission of The Macmillan Company from Richard Flacks, "Revolt of the Young Intelligentsia: Revolutionary Class-Consciousness in a Post-Scarcity America," in *The New American Revolution* edited by Roderick Aya and Norman Miller. Copyright © 1971 by The Free Press, a Division of The Macmillan Company.

From *Problems of an Industrial Society* by William A. Faunce. © 1968 by McGraw-Hill, Inc. Used with permission of McGraw-Hill Book Company.

Reprinted by permission of Charles Scribner's Sons from *The Protestant Ethic and the Spirit of Capitalism* by Max Weber. Translated by Talcott Parsons. (Grateful acknowledgment is also made of permission by the English publishers, George Allen & Unwin, Ltd., London.)

From *The Social Construction of Reality* by Peter L. Berger and Thomas Luckmann. Copyright © 1966 by Peter L. Berger and Thomas Luckmann. Reprinted by permission of Doubleday & Company, Inc. (Grateful acknowledgment is also made of permission by the English publishers, Penguin Books Limited, London.)

From *Vital Parts* first published in 1970 by the Richard W. Baron Publishing Co., Inc. Copyright © 1970 by Thomas Berger. Reprinted by permission of the Richard W. Baron Publishing Co., Inc. and Harold Matson Company, Inc.

INDEX